The Bridgestone food lover's guides to Ireland **The Shopper's Guide**

The Bridgestone
food lover's guides to Ireland:

The Shopper's Guide

JOHN McKENNA - SALLY McKENNA

ESTRAGON PRESS

First Published in Autumn 2001

by Estragon Press

Durrus

Co Cork

© Estragon Press

Text © John & Sally McKenna
The moral right of the authors has been asserted

ISBN 1 874076 40 5

Printed in Ireland by Colour Books Ltd

Written by John McKenna

Contributing Editors

Orla Broderick

Elizabeth Field

Caroline Workman

Publishing Editor: Sally McKenna

Editor: Judith Casey

Art Direction: Nick Cann

Illustrations: Aoife Wasser

Web: fluidedge.ie

For Sam McKenna

With thanks to

Colm Conyngham, Des Collins, Brian Condon, Frieda Forde,

Helen Kelleher, Sile Ginanne, Conor Cahill, Paul Willoughby,

Ian Vickery, Bernadette O'Shea, Paula Buckley, Judith Casey,

Maureen Daly, Colette Tobin, Catherine Tobin, Nick Cann, Pat Young,

Maurice Earls, Mike O'Toole, Ann Marie Tobin, Chris Carroll,

Paul Neilan, Ray Buckley, Gary Joyce, Kate and John Fraher

Bridgestone

...is the world's largest tyre and rubber manufacturer.

• Founded in Japan in 1931, it currently employs over 95,000 people in Europe, Asia and America and its products are sold in more than 150 countries. Its European plants are situated in France, Spain and Italy.

• Bridgestone manufacture tyres for a wide variety of vehicles from passenger cars and motorcycles, trucks and buses to giant earthmovers and aircraft.

• Many Japanese and European cars sold in Ireland have been fitted with Bridgestone tyres during manufacture and a host of exotic sports cars including Ferrari, Lamborghini, Porsche and Jaguar are fitted with Bridgestone performance tyres as original equipment.

• Bridgestone commercial vehicle tyres enjoy a worldwide reputation for superior cost per kilometre performance and its aircraft tyres are used by more than 100 airlines.

• In 1988 Bridgestone acquired the Firestone Tyre and Rubber Company combining the resources of both companies under one umbrella. This, coupled with an intensive research and development programme, has enabled Bridgestone to remain the world's most technologically advanced tyre company with testing centres in Japan, USA, Mexico and Italy.

• Bridgestone tyres are distributed in Ireland by Bridgestone/Firestone Ireland Limited, a subsidiary of the multinational Bridgestone Corporation. A wide range of tyres are stocked in its central warehouse and staff provide sales, technical and delivery services all over Ireland.

• Bridgestone tyres are available from tyre dealers throughout Ireland.

• Details of specialist Bridgestone and Firestone dealers can be found at www.firststop-eu.com.

FOR FURTHER INFORMATION:

BRIDGESTONE/FIRESTONE IRELAND LTD
Unit 4
Leopardstown Office Park,
Dublin 18
Tel: (01) 295 2844
Fax: (01) 295 2858

34 Hillsborough Road,
Lisburn
BT28 1AQ
Tel: 028 926 78331

website: www.bridgestone-eu.com

Introduction

Everyone is a food lover

We all love real food, local food, hand-made food, for simple, but deeply profound, reasons.

In discovering and enjoying real food, we can access a true culture, the culture of creativity and sharing, the culture of agrarianism and origin. Once upon a time, when lives were simpler and lived at slower paces, we took these things for granted. But today, we need real food to connect us in a true way to our own cultures. We need it to help us regain time in a true sense.

The writer Patience Gray, whose book "Honey from a Weed" is one of the most profound meditations on the culture of food ever written, has described how "in making things you make time your own", and that is exactly what the artisans described in this book do with their foods, each and every day of the year.

In enjoying these foods, we get the benefit of their time, we are conscious of their skills, their patience, their trueness, we are conscious of their artistry. At a time when commercialism dominates every aspect of our lives, the fruit of the work of the great artisans, the power of these people who work with food, is more valuable than ever, and more vital and important in our daily lives.

That people understand this need for real food, and respond to it, is more evident than ever today. The artisans and specialists described in this book are valued, appreciated and, in this way, they are truly "successful". Their success is not material, of course: it is much more important than that. They succeed because, in making time their own, they create a culture, the culture of real food. Lucky us, that we can all share it.

John and Sally McKenna
Durrus, Co Cork

Symbols

● We have always been resistant to the idea that there is a hierarchy involved in assessing and judging the best foods and food producers. We dislike the idea of Stars and Gongs, and the belief that at the top of the pile there is some food or some producer or some shop which is somehow 'the best'. For us, this is simply too reductivist, and denies many of the most interesting foods and food producers in Ireland their true value.

organic

● So, rather than establishing a free-for-all amongst the foods and the people described in this book, we have instead used the following symbols to illuminate the most pertinent character of the principal foods and food sellers featured. Please feel more than free to disagree with any or all of our designations! One man's revolutionary, after all, can be another's man's conservative.

artisan

traditional/regional

food revolutionary

a gift

don't miss it

i want it!

How to use this book

● To use this book, you need little more than an appetite and a sense of appreciation. If you have a sense of enquiry, so much the better, for then you will discover more and more of the wonderful foods we describe.

● Shopping for interesting foods has never been easier in Ireland. More of the best foods are now more available than ever before, and the growth of street markets has seen a happy situation where producers sell direct to their happy customers. Some producers have made assiduous use of the internet to both increase their business and to retain control of how they sell their foods. Wherever possible, we have given e-mail and web details, and this is an exciting and progressive way forward for many artisans.

● Supermarkets have also made serious efforts to improve the number of specialist and artisan foods they sell, but for us there is still nothing nicer than making the effort to go to a specialist market and buying the foods direct from the grower or producer. Supermarkets believe that they are offering the best choice possible, but in reality this is often illusory. What supermarkets do not offer is a range of choices, they do not offer rare varieties of vegetables, true artisan imported products, difficult to obtain foods and wines. Supermarkets are mainstream, and to find the best foods you often have to walk on the wild side. Taking that walk on the wild side is one of the most exciting cultural explorations you can make, for it will reveal the true culture of Ireland's food.

● Most of the shops described in The Shopper's Guide keep fairly standard hours, opening from Monday to Saturday for most of the day. With the markets we describe, it is always best to arrive early to get the best choice: some of these country markets are virtually sold out in 10 minutes! So, join in the free-for-all, it's pure fun.

Contents

Dublin great city shops

● **Avoca Handweavers**
The newest Avoca temple to hip consumerism has an
spiffing shop in the basement selling lots of excellent
breads and choice deli foods, many of them made
by Ireland's leading artisans to be sold under the
Avoca label. Unmissable.
(Suffolk St, D2, Tel: (01) 677 4215 avoca.ie)

● **The Big Cheese Co.**
David Brown's excellent shop has a somewhat misleading name: yes,
it does sell a fantastic selection of cheeses from all over the world,
but it is the hard-to-find imported and kosher foods which you will
also find here that make it such an important address.
(Trinity St, D2, Tel: (01) 671 1399)

● **Caviston's Seafood**
The original Caviston's deli and restaurant is in Glasthule,
on the southside of town, but the Epicurean Mall
branch of the Caviston family's superlative fish
business is vital as the home to the freshest fish in the
city. Also a cult place to have lunch whilst you ponder
what manner of fishy fishy or crustacea takes your fancy.
(59 Glasthule Rd, Sandycove, Dun Laoghaire, Tel: (01) 280 9245;
Epicurean Food Mall, Tel: (01) 878 2289 cavistons.com)

● **Crème de la Crème**
The Ouchbakou brothers' patisserie is magnificent,
executed with the sort of jaw-dropping skills which great
French patissiers revel in. Unrestrainedly indulgent and
wickedly magnificent and not to be missed.
(Epicurean Food Mall, D1, Tel: (01) 836 4202)

Dunne & Crescenzi

Vital Italian ingredients of seriously good artisan provenance can be found in this brilliant store: super polenta; great arborio; good oils and wines; lovely artisan preserves. And do take a break and have some salami and olives and a glass of wine as you shop: you deserve it.
(14 Sth Frederick St, D2, Tel: (01) 677 3815)

The Gallic Kitchen

Sarah Webb remains the great baker of Dublin city, after more than a decade at the oven, and her cooked foods-to-go are peerless: salmon and broccoli plait; basil and mozzarella tart; fantastic potato cakes; great sausage rolls; spicy burritos; superb sweet baking. The shop, with its pair of little counters and stools, is also a great lunch stop, and Ms Webb also offers a vital catering service for dinner parties. On Saturday mornings, the Gallic Kitchen cycles down to Temple Bar Market to feed the masses with great food: on no account should you miss the finnan haddie quiches, which are simply sublime. But then, the sublime is what Sarah Webb does.
(49 Francis St, D8, Tel: (01) 454 4912)

COOK'S TOOLS

■ Kitchen Complements
The success of Ann McNamee's shop is based on the fact that Ann tirelessly searches out exciting new tools and toys for the serious cook; every time you come in to 'Complements, there is some fine new thing which demands you buy it. As well as the newer innovations, the classics of the kitchen from Rösle to Global are all here. Serious knowledge and judgement are also on offer, and they have a fine range of classes and special promotions running frequently.
(Chatham St, D2, Tel: (01) 677 0734, k.compl@oceanfree.net)

■ Sweeney O'Rourke
Don't let its somewhat "trade only" style put you off walking into Sweeney O'Rourke, for ordinary decent members of the public can shop here too, even though most of the stock is dedicated to servicing the professional kitchen. Friendly staff are very knowledgeable and, when your Dualit toaster burns through its heating frames, this is where you will find replacements.
(34 Pearse St, D2, Tel: (01) 677 7212 sweeneyorourke.com)

Dublin – City shops

● The Good Food Store

Vanessa Clarke's lovely little shop on Pembroke Lane, just off Lower Baggot Street, now has a sister store in Ringsend as well as an outlet in the Epicurean Mall. All are packed with must-have! foods, from organic vegetables to rare relishes and meats, and Ms Clarke really understands and appreciates her supplies and her suppliers. Excellent sandwiches will keep you going as you hoover up everything good in the store, and everything is good: 'We only sell good food,' says Ms Clarke. Do ask about their hamper service, which is especially imaginative and quite different from most hamper offers.
(7 Pembroke Lane, D4,
Tel: (01) 667 5656, Ringsend (01) 668 4514)

● La Maison des Gourmets

The prices are high in Olivier Quenet and Nicolas Boutin's neat traiteur, particularly for the cooked foods on sale, but the quality of the French foods in which La Maison specialises means the specialities are usually worth it. Good patisserie and breads from their own bakery are a big attraction and perhaps the backbone of the shop – their croissants in particular are excellent – and they even import Poilane bread, admittedly at a high price! The most recent innovation has been a rather nice tea room where one can enjoy their splendid baking.
Look out for the Neuhaus chocolates.
(15 Castle Market, D2,
Tel: (01) 672 7258)

Revolution!

Sheridan's Cheesemongers

The Sheridan brothers and Fiona Corbett revolutionised cheese selling in Ireland, nothing less. Their in-depth knowledge of every Irish artisan farmhouse cheese, which they sell at the very peak of maturity, is matched by their skill in sourcing superb Continental cheeses and lots of other loveable delicacies from Italy, France and –

Laragh Stuart Foods

'Slow Food – Not Fast Food' is how Laragh Stuart describes her splendid deli business, which operates out of the George's Street arcade. Excellent preserves, relishes and sauces, and fantastic soups and sandwiches to go make it a great lunchtime spot also.
(George's St Arcade, D2, Tel: (01) 617 4827)

Magills

Kim Condon's deli was here long before Dubliners got hooked onto the food lovin' experience, and it remains one of the great addresses for sourcing good foods: look out for Stone Oven breads from Wicklow in particular.
(14 Clarendon St, D2, Tel: (01) 671 3830)

The Olive Green Food Co

Marina and Justin's smashing food stall-cum-shop in the George's Street Market is indispensable for rarities such as Turkish delight; porcini oil; smoked garlic; organic sweets and a fine selection of organic vegetables, as well as good grains and pulses.
(George's St Arcade, D2, olivegreen@indigo.ie)

Temple Bar Bakery

Jimmy White's happy and friendly bakery on Pudding Row (ho,ho) is a key Temple Bar address, and the baking is homey and rather moreish, with everything baked from scratch. 'No mixes,' says Jimmy, 'we make it and bake it.' Good on 'em.
(Essex Street West, Tel: (01) 672 9882).

Seamus Sheridan's newest enthusiasm – Portugal. Buy whatever they recommend. When it comes to cheese – these guys have visited and made cheese with virtually all the Irish artisan cheesemakers, so they know everything about their cheeses – but in particular don't miss the oatcakes, the truffle oil, their particularly excellent Parmesan, and the fennel salamis which they import direct from Italy. A vital address. (11 Sth Anne St, D2, Tel: (01) 679 3143) sheridans cheesemongers@eircom.net

Temple Bar Market

In a few short years, the Temple Bar Saturday Market has blossomed into one of the city's don't miss it! destinations. The number of producers selling at the market in Meetinghouse Square has grown steadily, and the sense of camaraderie amongst the traders is as great an attraction as the fantastic foods they sell. If you haven't toured the market and snapped up goodies hither and thither, you haven't done Dublin. Open 9am-6pm each Saturday.

PRESERVES
● The Real Olive Co

Tobias Simmonds has been one of the most important food specialists in Ireland during the last decade, and not just because he is the man who converted Ireland to the delights of eating olives. No, what Toby has done is to support each and every market he can find, wherever it may be, with his team of whirlwind stall operators. So from Castletownbere to Temple Bar, via Limerick and Killarney and Galway the Real Olive Co will be there, thronged as usual.

● Olvi Oils

Miriam Griffith's splendid flavoured oils and pastes are quite unique, and their special qualities have been garnering them major prizes at fine food shows recently. Don't miss the green olive paste.

VEGETARIAN
● The Pure Vegetarian

Richie Crook brings in vegetables from his farm and homemade chutneys.

BREAD & CHEESE

● Sheridans
The revolutionary cheesemongers market stall: expect the impeccable.

● Burren Gold Traders
Excellent cheeses and milk from the West Coast.

● Silke Cropp
Silke Cropp is one of the great market stalwarts, driving down from Cavan each Saturday with her beautiful farmhouse cheeses, Corleggy and Drumlin, to join in the craic. Look out for the fresh cheeses.

● Noirin Kearney
Fine domestic breads, cakes, tartlets, scones.

● Piece of Cake
Darko Marjanovic makes great Italian bread & cakes and neat filo pies.

● Jenny McNally
Jenny brings a range of good things in from the family farm in Naul in North Dublin, including vegetables, preserves, yogurt and French bread.

The Cow's Lane Market:

This brand new venture in the Old City has been set up by Temple Bar Properties to concentrate on suppliers of raw ingredients. Some of the initial producers include: Marc Michel's Organic Life and Denis Healy's organic vegetables, both from County Wicklow, and there are more fantastic organics from Absolutely Organic. Mary MacRory has organic strawberries in season, whilst Frank Hederman sells his awesomely fine smoked foods – don't miss the smoked mussels. The Abbey Cheese Co from County Laois has cheeses and clever preserved cheeses for salads, all organic, whilst John McInerney's St Martin shellfish company from County Clare will sell you as many oysters as you need for a maximum zinc fix, along with lobsters, crab and fish.

Dublin – Temple Bar Market

CHOCOLATES & CAKES

● **Wabbit Fudge Co**
Bridgit Goulet Diskin's fudge is delectable.

● **Chez Emily**
Helena Hemerych makes
fabulous handmade
chocolates: a real treat.

● **Claudia's Buns**
Claudia Medina McNamara
sells fine cakes and buns.

JUICES & BERRIES

● **Richard & Carolina Brennan**
Fruit and vegetable juices which seem to
be just the thing to cope with that
hangover.

● **Llewellyn's Apple Farm**
Pick up some of the cute green bottles
with their bright labels, and maybe get a
hot glass of juice to perk you up. Look out
for their cider.

COOKED FOOD TO GO

● **Miss Sushi**
Margaret Scully sells her
fine sushi at the Temple
Bar Market as well as the
Epicurean Mall.

● **Gallic Kitchen**
Peerless pastries from Dublin's Baking
Queen; the agony of choosing just what
you want to eat is allayed by the sheer
pleasure which lies ahead when you have
made your mind up.

WORLD FOOD

ITALIAN, SPANISH & MEXICAN

• **Marco Bartomucci**
Look out for specialist
Italian dishes and
ingredients from Marco.

• **Flavours of Mexico**
Gus and Theresa
Hernandez make the very
best Mexican condiments
you can buy in Ireland.
The jalapenos en
escabeche are
thunderously good, the
Mexican catsup is
dreamy and spicy, the
chilli oil is a fiery blast,
and there are even
champagne habaneros.
And if you fancy a stroll,
make your way up to
their Mero Mero café in
Stoneybatter for more of
the real thing with ace
tacos and burritos.

• **Florence & Damian**
Cusack bake fine bread
for the market and sell
Italian coffee: a straight
up caffeine fix is just
what you need

• **Spanish Tapas**: some
paella and a little tortilla
to go.

MEAT
● Ed Hick

No, we can't resist the smell of grilling sausages from
Ed Hick's barbecue stall either. One in a bun with
mustard, please, and two packs to go. Some of the
very best sausages that you will find in Ireland: don't
miss the Wicklow venison when it is in season, and

don't miss the wine and garlic and the bratwurst and the merguez.
Hell, don't miss any of them!

Some of Ed's Gourmet sausages include:

**Chorizo... Italian Salsiccia... Merguez... Cajun Sausages...
Wine & Garlic Sausage... Venison Sausage... Kolbasa... Boerewoers...**

● Pat Cremin

Organic deer and lamb and good chickens are
brought down from Longford by Pat each Saturday
morning, and sold with helpful, benign advice by the
man himself.

● Hugh Robson

Hugh Robson's organic meat comes from his own farm,
and it is superlative. Look out, in particular, for the blood
puddings made by Sarah Robson and, if you want to
square the circle on the Robson family empire, take
yourself up to the funky Ely Wine Bar, on Ely Place at the
end of Merrion Row in Dublin 2, where son Erik features the foods on
his menu: we'll have the organic brunch please, Erik.

Great Irish foods to find in the supermarkets:
CHOCCA MOCCA CHOCOLATES

Dublin southside

BLACKROCK

● ● ● ● ● ● ● ● ● ● ● ● ● ● ● ● ● ● ●

● Rosanna, Joannie and Leslie make the most spiffingly gorgeous cakes you will find in Dublin in their shop **Cakes & Co**. The sugar craft these women weave is so fine that it can seem that the cakes are purely decorative, but they are also quite delicious. They will make a cake to any design and specification you wish, and Cakes & Co cakes are just about the best treat you can buy: these really make a special occasion extra special.
(25 Rock Hill, Blackrock Village, Tel: (01) 283 6544)

● We rather like the feel and layout of the **Roches Stores** flagship store, and they sell lots of good things. Do note that their Henry St branch is a vital address in the centre city.
(Blackrock Shopping Centre, Tel: (01) 288 5391)

● Fergal Quinn's **Superquinn** chain of super-markets has expanded steadily over the last decade, with stores now found as far afield as Waterford and Kilkenny. The flagship Blackrock store is many southsiders favourite big store, and whilst the Superquinn team are just about as hard-nosed as any other major retailer, they do instigate useful initiatives that make the stores valuable. For example, they work hard to mature farmhouse cheeses, and to sell them in peak condition, something other supermarkets haven't a clue about. The result of these initiatives, of course, is increased sales, so they aren't philanthropists, but they do make the effort. Their wine stores are also good – and feature a very interesting annual sale – and they still make a pretty decent sausage after all these years.
(Blackrock Shopping Centre, Tel: (01) 283 8274)

● One of the most interesting **SuperValu** stores is the one run by Damien Kiernan in Mount Merrion, up the hill and across the motorway from Blackrock. This is an excellent and superbly run shop and a real local treasure, for they understand and appreciate the foods made by many of Ireland's finest specialist producers. Whilst the city SuperValu stores are often not as interesting as some of the country stores, they are always worth exploring.

(Mount Merrion, Tel: (01) 288 1014

ETHNIC DUBLIN

The area around Parnell Street and Moore Street in D1 has been excitingly colonised by many new ethnic shops.

■ The original and best known of the shops catering to the African communities is John Bankole's **Tropical Store** on Parnell Street, which opened in 1997.

■ Since then, others have joined in this little strip of exotica; **Joyceanna** on Moore Street opened in 2000, run by Steve and Deborah Oladeji.

■ Frank Allen has opened **Slavyanskaya Lavka**, which specialises in Baltic and Russian foods.

■ **Azure Holdings** is for Chinese foods and there are many other stalls selling ethnic foods in the **Moore Street indoor market.**

■ In the centre of the city, **The Asia Market** on Drury Street is still the best ethnic store in the city, the place where you will find everything Asian that can be used for cooking and eating, from woks to bak choi, from noodles of many hues all the way to frozen fish the like of which you have never seen before.

■ There is also the **Asian Food Store** on Camden Street.

■ **Erlich's** is a kosher butcher's shop on Camden Street.

■ **The Islamic Centre** on South Circular Road also has a store selling specialist foods.

■ For Japanese and Pacific rim cooking, then **AYA** at the rere of Brown Thomas on Clarendon Street has a good selection of ethnic foods for sale in its shop, so if you are determined to make sushi, start here.

■ The newest branches - **AYA 2 Go** in Donnybrook and the **AYA Deli** in the IFSC in the financial quarter – also sell some specialist foods as well as food-to-go.

Dublin – Southside

DONNYBROOK

● ● ● ● ● ● ● ● ● ● ● ● ● ● ● ● ●

● If you can't find it in **Roy Fox**, whatever it may be, then it hasn't been grown, reared, produced or cooked by anyone. This extraordinary shop, tucked just off the main strip of Donnybrook near to the rugby ground, is the closest Dublin gets to a souk-meets-bazaar all under one (tiny!) roof. Visit on Sunday afternoon, when the atmosphere is like a food lover's club.
(49a Main St, Donnybrook, Tel: (01) 269 2892)

● **Molloys of Donnybrook** are game specialists, as well as a good source of fresh fish.
(Donnybrook Rd, D4, Tel: (01) 269 1678)

● **Terroirs** is a wine shop, on the strip in Donnybrook, but it's a lot more than that: Terroirs is where you come to buy a gift for a food lover, for Sean and Francoise Gilley have the most superlative selection of treats you can find anywhere in town. Fantastic discrimination, and the very best packaging in Dublin, make this a vital address. The wines, of course, are as choice and quaffable as you will get, and there is nowhere else quite like Terroirs. Brilliant. Mrs Gilley also dresses the most beautiful window displays to be found in the city: just ogle those delectable displays.
(103 Morehampton Rd, D4, Tel: (01) 667 1311, Fax: 667 1312, terroirs.ie)

Edible gifts from Terroirs:

'The number one present would be single estate olive oil. We always wrap it beautifully if it's to be a gift, and of course it's a present that people will actually use – Ornellaia olive oil is a real favourite.

'Foie Gras makes a lovely present and we recommend a Coteaux de Layon or a Bonnezeaux wine, both of which work very well with it.

'Pouchkine tea is also a popular gift. It's similar to Earl Grey, and the Darjeeling from the Margaret Hope garden is popular.

'Otherwise, Armagnac from your year of birth, because you're sure of it holding in the bottle.'

Dundrum:

• Mulberry Market

Now, here is something exciting. Kelly and Jackie Spillane, who created the excellent Morley's range of sauces and preserves, have established a purpose-built shop specialising in artisan foods and interesting wines, right in the middle of a 40-acre working farm, in suburban Dublin.

The original idea was, essentially, to have a farm gate shop, but Mulberry Market has moved beyond that to become home to farmhouse cheeses, organic foods, local crafts and fresh breads. Kelly Spillane is a seriously clever food lover, and this is a key address on the southside.
(Airfield House, Upper Kilmacud Road, Dundrum, D14
Tel: (01) 296 0212)

MARKET!

The Dublin Food Co-Op
On Saturday mornings, people queue up at the Dublin Food Co-Op to buy carrots. Not just any carrots, of course. They are queueing up to buy Penny Lange's bio-dynamically grown carrots, dug up at Ballinroan Farm in County Wicklow and driven into Pearse Street by the lady herself. Creating this sort of discrimination amongst its customers, and offering them access to fantastic foods of all manner, has been the great gift of Pauric Cannon and his team at the Co-Op, and they have been doing it for almost two decades now. This has been a truly revolutionary venture, an exercise in offering a different way to source and shop for foods, combined with a healthy dose of agit-prop politics. Teams of helpers put the produce into bags, volunteers take your money, and if you wish to get involved in the Co-Op then there is a rich fabric of society to embrace. If you just want to find great organic and bio-dynamic foods sold by great producers from around the country and don't wish to partake of the altruism, then the Co-Op remains one of the most vital addresses in the city.
(St Andrew's Centre, Pearse St,
Tel: (01) 873 0451, 9.30am-3pm Saturday)

Dublin – Southside

DUN LAOGHAIRE & GLASTHULE

● Bloomfield's Foodhall is one of the **Tesco** flagship stores and stocks an interesting assortment of specialist foods, amidst all the quotidian stuff. This branch, and the large Tesco on the Merrion Road, are their two best shops. The fish counter and wine shop are both good.
(Dun Laoghaire, Tel: (01) 230 1863) (Merrion Rd, Tel: (01) 283 8274)

● In the large and unattractive Dun Laoghaire shopping centre, a popular address is **Ballycumber Meats**, whose meat comes from their own farms.
(Dun Laoghaire Shopping Centre, Tel: (01) 280 3010)

● Food lovers are often to be found during the week on **Dun Laoghaire pier** all buying fresh fish from Helen, Mary, Geraldine and Matt at the fish stall at the Coal Harbour.
(Dun Laoghaire Pier, Tel: (01) 280 5936)

● Glasthule is the true Gourmet Grotto on the southside. **Caviston's** deli and fish shop is one of the finest delis you can find, and every interesting Irish artisan food makes its way here. Steven and Peter Caviston manage one of the glories of Irish food, and when making a pilgrimage do make sure to try to have lunch – but book in advance or you won't get in.
(59 Glasthule Rd, Dun Laoghaire, Tel: (01) 280 9245, Fax: 284 4054, caviston@indigo.ie, cavistons.com)
● The other key addresses are **Mitchell's** wine shop
(54 Glasthule Rd, Sandycove, Tel: (01) 230 2301 – see the entry on

Great Irish foods to find in the supermarkets:
ST KILLIAN BRIE

wine merchants) and **O'Toole's** butchers' shop, where Tom O'Connor sells superlative organic meats. The village atmosphere of little Glasthule makes every visit here a real treat.
(1b Glasthule Rd, Tel: (01) 284 1125. mitchellandson.com)

● And just a little bit up the hill from Glasthule you will find Ed Hick's fantastic butcher's shop, **Hick's Of Sallynoggin**, just in front of the green at Woodpark. Ed Hick understands the art of butchering better than anyone, and everything he makes and sells is fantastic, above all the specialist sausages and the benchmark kassler, his real signature creation. You can't live in Dublin and not shop here, and do note that Mr Hick is also a stalwart of the Temple Bar Market in the centre city, where he has a stall every Saturday.
(Wood Park, Sallynoggin, Tel: (01) 285 4430, pinkpig.com)

B E S T   B A G E L S

Domini and Peaches Kemp attract the biggest queues in the city every day for their delectable, seriously yumola bagels.
So, what are the five best-selling bagels in **Itsabagel?**

• **CLUB BAGEL**
Everything bagel with free-range chicken, crispy bacon, brie, red onion marmalade, lettuce, tomato, mayo

• **MOUNTAINEER**
Sesame bagel, ham, turkey, Swiss, cheese, lettuce, tomato, honey Dijon, and mayo

• **DELUXE WITH THE WORKS**
Poppy seed bagel, cream cheese, smoked Irish salmon, capers and red onion

• **GOURMET VEGGIE**
Sun-dried tomato bagel, goat's cheese, roasted red peppers, humous, tapenade, red onion marmalade, lettuce and butter

• **ITSAREUBEN**
Pumpernickel bagel, pastrami, Swiss cheese, caramelised onions, their own 1000 Island Dressing.
(Epicurean Mall, D1, Tel: (01) 874 0486; Dun Laoghaire Pavilion, itsabagel.com)

Dublin – Southside

RANELAGH, RATHMINES & RATHGAR

● ● ● ● ● ● ● ● ● ● ● ● ● ● ● ● ●

● Locals love Catriona Norton's busy and buzzy **A Taste of Italy**, on Dunville Avenue, which squeezes the most amazing range of Italian foods and wines into what is just a tiny store. The local secret, here, is the excellent bread – 'the best in Dublin', the locals argue. Thoughtfully, they are also open on Sunday mornings so you can get a proper brunch together.
(37 Dunville Ave, D6, Tel: (01) 497 3411)

● On the same strip as A Taste of Italy is one of the most interesting independent supermarkets in Dublin. **Morton's** is a fabulous shop, packed with great raw ingredients, a good selection of wines, and excellent cooked food to go.
Fantastic staff make this a truly pleasurable place to shop, a store which has a true neighbourhood spirit.
(15 Dunville Ave, D6, Tel: (01) 497 1254)

● On the strip of Ranelagh, Jimmy Redmond's stonkingly good wine shop and off-licence is a vital local address. The range in **Redmond's** is only brilliant, including quite a few rare wines if you want to buy someone a treat. If you are rushing somewhere at evening-time, you can even get your wine chilled fast.
(25 Ranelagh Village, D6, Tel: (01) 496 0552)

● And just at the Triangle, Brendan **Gammell's** deli is a good spot for breads and cooked foods courtesy of the Butler's Pantry team.
(33 Ranelagh, D6, Tel: (01) 496 2311)

● In Rathmines, Terry and Breda Lilburn's **Fothergills** delicatessen is one of the original Dublin delis, and still one of the very best. Fantastic sweet baking draws in the crowds (locals actually get desserts put into their own crockery!) but everything in here is good,

Great Irish foods to find in the supermarkets:
DUNBARRA CHEESE

chosen with care, and sold with great patience and knowledge: once again it is the true neighbourhood service that brings you back to Fothergills time after time.
(141 Upper Rathmines Rd, D6, Tel: (01) 496 2511)

● In Rathgar, the **Gourmet Store** is a charmingly old-fashioned shop, the like of which is increasingly rare, (Rathgar, D6, Tel: (01) 497 0365), whilst another vital local address is the excellent **The Vintry** wine shop, where Evelyn Jones and her team run a great operation.
(102 Rathgar Rd, D6, Tel: (01) 490 5477)

TERENURE

●●●●●●●●●●●●●●●●●●

● You can find John Downey's, **Downey's of Terenure** spiced beef in some Dublin supermarkets, but it's great fun to visit the original shop at the traffic lights in Terenure. Lots of specialities, apart from the spiced beef, make this a key destination; try the organic meats and the smoked lamb.
(Terenure Cross, D6, Tel: (01) 490 9239)

● **Danny O'Toole** began selling organic meat when it was neither fashionable nor profitable. Now that it is both, this great butcher gets the accolades he deserves for his foresight in concentrating on meat which is reared on Irish organic farms. The meat is superb, thanks to meticulous sourcing and, vitally, proper hanging. There is also a second branch in Glasthule on the southside.
(138 Terenure Rd Nth, D6, Tel: (01) 490 5457)

Dublin northside

CLONTARF

● **Nolan's** is a compact, spotless independent supermarket on Vernon Avenue and is prized by locals for their excellent choice of organic meat and vegetables and frozen Butler's Pantry section. It's an Aladdin's cave for more unusual produce and has saved many's a local's life many a time.
(49 Vernon Ave, D3, Tel: (01) 833 6929)

HOWTH

● There are any number of fish sellers on the pier at Howth, but at any time of the day you will find the biggest queue in **Nicky's Plaice** (ouch!), where Nicky McLoughlin and his family sell the freshest fish you can find on the northside. It's a tiny place – virtually a lean-to cabin, really – but the devoted punters don't care about anything other than the spankingly fresh fish.
(Howth West Pier, Tel: (01) 832 3557)

MALAHIDE

● Aisling Boyle's **The Foodware Store** opened its doors in March of 2001 and has quickly become a Northside phenomenon, supplying really sassy and well understood food to delighted food lovers. The soups are great, the cheeses are from Sheridans, the salads are really

funky (you choose 'em, she dresses 'em), and whether it's something groovy like Moroccan lamb tagine or something homey such as honey baked ham or fish pie or sausage rolls, it's all done beautifully. Fine selection of wines, and altogether a life-saver for folk for miles around.
(19 Old Street, Malahide, Tel: (01) 845 1830)

SMITHFIELD

● ● ● ● ● ● ● ● ● ● ● ● ● ●

● **The Corporation Market** isn't just trade only, although that accounts for most of its business, but you will see discriminating shoppers here, carefully picking out the best things to buy then heading to **Paddy's Place** for a mug of tea and a bacon sandwich.
(Smithfield, D7, Tel: (01) 873 5130)

● Judy Davis and Richard Baker have been making their glamorous and funky range of **Lime and Lemongrass** foods since 1995, and whilst they are widely distributed via supermarkets and stores, such as Avoca Handweavers, their shop is the best place to see the entire range of relishes, sauces, dressings and dips. Good stuff for time-poor folk.
(2-3 Mary's Abbey, D7, Tel: (01) 872 2965 lemongrass@eircom.net limeandlemongrass.com)

● We have all gotten all chi-chi about Italian foods these days, but back in the days when it was dried pasta and 2-litre bottles of Bove, **Little Italy** was a life-saver. It's still a vital store for Arborio rice, dried porcini and other staples.
(North King St, D7, Tel: (01) 872 5208)

We asked The Foodware Store... What are you most popular salad combos?

▣ **Penne pasta with sundried tomatoes and basil pesto dressing**
▣ **Couscous salad with roasted vegetables and balsamic dressing**
▣ **Chick-pea salad with cumin, coriander and chilli dressing**
▣ **Grated carrot, courgette and coriander salad**
▣ **Mixed bean salad with sweet pepper and lemon dressing**

Dublin

CCTT

Where we have all been: Can't Cook, Too Tired...
Put together the basic facts about city living – longer
working hours, longer traffic jams, two partners working all
week, little time to cook – and you put together the recipe
for food-to-take-home. But we don't mean processed food
that goes from a freezer into a microwave; we mean real
cooking. It amazes us that more restaurants don't sell their
food to take away, but it will happen, we reckon. The
following, meantime, have answered the call for food-to-
take-home for CCTT's who want something real and tasty.

● AYA

Pioneering Japanese food to go, which can be ordered in advance by
telephone, or through their website. A terrific range of sushi is offered.
Delivery in the locality only.
(rear Brown Thomas, Clarendon St; 51a Main St, Donnybrook, D4;
IFSC Custom House Square, Mayor St, D1, Tel: (01) 677 1544, aya.ie)

● Douglas Food Co

The DFC is not merely an excellent traiteur, but is vitally important
because Grainne Murphy prepares food for people on special diets.
Working closely with dieticians, meals are prepared for those
watching cholesterol, and for coeliacs. A retail shop has recently
opened in Dalkey, just down from The Queens.
(53 Donnybrook Rd, D4, Tel: (01) 269 4066) (14 Castle St, Dalkey, Tel:
(01) 284 7184 grainne@thedouglasfoodco.ie)

● Gruel

Ben Gorman describes his cooking in Gruel as 'short order cooking –
but nice', and their 'gourmet tv dinners' are just the ticket for cctt city

folk: let them do it for you, they can do it better.
(Dame St, D2, Tel: (01) 670 8236)

● La Maison des Gourmets
Classical French-style food and whilst the prices are high, the quality
and expertise is undoubted. (15 Castle Market, D2, Tel: (01) 672 7258)

● The Butler's Pantry
Eileen Bergin's shops pioneered food-to-go in Dublin, and their
second branch in Donnybrook again brings real, handmade food to
more folk on the southside.
(97b Morehampton Rd, D'brook, Tel: (01) 660 8490; 53 Mount
Merrion Ave, D4, Tel: (01) 288 3443)

● **Superquinn** have introduced prepared meals in both their
Blackrock store and their expanding **Super Q** chain of shops in
garage forecourts around Dublin.
(Blackrock Shopping Centre, Tel: (01) 283 8274)

● **Morton's of Ranelagh** does an enormous trade with its cooked
food to bring home. (15 Dunville Ave, D6, Tel: (01) 497 1254)

● **The Bombay Pantry** in Glenageary has been home to the best
Indian food you can find. The new branch in Rathmines brings this
excellent cooking to city dwellers
(Glenageary Shopping Centre, Tel: (01) 285 6683. 14 Rathgar Road,
Rathmines, Tel: (01) 496 9695)

PLEASE MAY I HAVE MORE?

Six popular soups from Ben & Mark's Gruel:
▓ Tomato Soup with pasta, goat's cheese and basil pesto
▓ Caldo Verde
▓ Lemon Chicken Broth
▓ Smoked Haddock Chowder
▓ Thai Prawn and Coconut Soup
▓ Andalucian Fisherman's Soup made with Cod & Orange

Dublin

Drink THIS

Dublin is a good city in which to shop for wine, and the best wine merchants combine knowledge with excellent service. Whilst the supermarket chains work hard to polish their lists, the specialists still have an edge.

● In the city centre, **Berry Bros & Rudd** run a beautiful store on Harry Street, so beautiful that it's a treat just to linger here. But the wines are excellent, and the service is sharp and informed.
(4 Harry St, D2, Tel: (01) 677 3444)

● In Temple Bar, the **Vaughan Johnson** shop is a specialist in South African wines, and it's an intimate, clubbable space with lots of nice surprises amongst the crates and shelves. (Essex St East, Tel: (01) 671 5355) On the other side of the river, **Layden Fine Wines** in the Epicurean Mall is a sweet little wine shop and they are working hard to establish their reputation.
(Epicurean Food Hall, Lwr Liffey St, D1, Tel: (01) 878 2221 laydenfinewines.com)

● **Findlater's** of Hatch Street has recently been taken over by one of the big drinks consortiums, so one can expect developments on the shelves of this cavernous store.
 (The Harcourt St Vaults, 10 Upr Hatch St, D2, sales@findlaters.com, Tel: (01) 475 1699)

● **Mitchell's** of Kildare Street has a new energy about it these days, and has recently moved back into wholesaling once again. Their list has a new dynamism as newer wines are added, and the Kildare street shop is quite gorgeous. Their second branch in the gourmet grotto of Glasthule is splendid and fair play to a company, established almost 200 years ago, in maintaining such a sharp focus. (21 Kildare St, D2, mitchellandson.com, mitchkst@indigo.ie)

● Another renewed company is **O'Brien's Wines**, who have outlets in and around the city, with the leading branch in Donnybrook, and who are continually expanding and introducing new wines under the direction of David Whelehan. (30-32 Donnybrook Rd, D4 Tel: (01) 269 3139, Fax: (01) 269 3033, obrienswines.ie)

● **Oddbins** range of wines is superb, the enthusiasm and savvy of their staff legendary. (17 Uppr Baggot St, D4, Tel: (01) 667 3033, 23 Rock Hill, Blackrock, Co Dublin, Tel: (01) 278 3844, 125 Braemor Rd, Churchtown, D14, Tel: (01) 296 3111, 360 Clontarf Rd, D3, Tel: (01) 833 1653, oddbins.com)

● On the southside, **Terroirs** in Donnybrook is not just one of the city's best wine shops, it is one of the city's best shops. If you are looking for something rare and hard to source for a special occasion, then this is the first port of call. (103 Morehampton Rd, D4, Tel: (01) 667 1311, Fax: 667 1312, terroirs.ie)

● **McCabe's** on Mount Merrion Avenue has a fantastic range of wines, and also boasts one of the best wine clubs you can find, with an enterprising series of classes each year, and also a singles wine club! (51-55 Mount Merrion Ave, Blackrock, Co Dublin, Tel: (01) 288 2037, Fax: (01) 288 3447, mccabeswines.com)

● **Searson's** of Monkstown is one of the best loved wine merchants in the country. Frank and Charles Searson are specialists in en primeur offers for claret and also in re-emerging regions such as Spain: their Spanish list is fantastic, the shop is a delight. (Monkstown Crescent, Tel: (01) 280 0405, Fax: (01) 280 4771, info@searsons.com)

Dublin Wine Shops

● Also on the southside, there is a smart new **Bubble Brothers** store in Dun Laoghaire, which is a great haunt to discover Billy Forrester's newest enthusiasm, as well as some excellent champagnes. (116 Lower Georges St, Dun Laoghaire, Tel: (01) 230 4117, bubblebrothers.com)

● For something off the beaten track, then do hunt down Conor Richardson's company, **Burgundy Direct** a delightfully idiosyncratic little list. (8 Monaloe Way, Blackrock, Tel: (01) 289 6615, Fax: (01) 289 8470, burgundy@indigo.ie)

● For Italian wines check out **Dunne & Crescenzi** on South Frederick Street for real Italian artisan wines. (14 Sth Frederick St, D2, Tel: (01) 677 3815, crescenz@iol.ie)

● Look for hard-to-find little clarets on Ronan Foster's list at **Best Cellars**, a small, select choice. (4 Knocklyon Rd, Templeogue, D14, Tel: (01) 494 6508, Fax: (01) 495 0592, info@bestcellars.ie)

● In Dalkey, check out Pamela Cooney's lovely wine shop, **On The Grapevine**. St. Patrick's Road, Tel: (01) 235 3054.

WINE ON LINE

■ www.barryfitzwilliam.com

■ www.bbr.ie

■ www.berrybrothers.com

■ www.bestcellars.ie

■ www.compendiumwines.com

■ www.directwine.co.uk

■ www.ewine.ie

■ www.findlaters.com

■ www.fineorganicwines.com

■ www.irelandonwine.com

■ www.jnwine.com

■ www.karwig-wines.ie

■ www.laydenfinewines.com

■ www.mccabeswine.com

■ www.molloys.com

■ www.obrienswines.ie

■ www.oddbins.com

■ www.onthecase.ie

■ www.searsons.com

■ www.thewineroom.ie

■ www.waterfordwinevault.com

■ www.wineworks.ie

Juices smoothies and wraps to go

● **Itsabagel** Organic fruit and vegetable juices and homemade lemonade along with the famous bagels.
(Epicurean Mall, D1, Tel: (01) 874 0486; Dun Laoghaire Pavilion, itsabagel.com)

● **The Joose Bar** City Squeezes, (make up your own combos), Smoothies and Juices.
(7a Poolbeg St, D2,
Tel: (01) 679 9611 Fax: 01-679 9642, www.joosebar.com)

● **Juice** Juice originated the fashion for vegetable juices in this late-night contemporary vegetarian venue.
(South St Georges St, D2,
Tel : 01 475 7856)

● **Nude** Originators of smoothies in Dublin, and still the best. The only place (we know of) to get real wheatgrass shots.

And their wraps are great too.
(21 Suffolk St, D2, Tel: (01) 672 5577)

● **The Milk Bar** The best rolls, wraps, juices and soups in Dublin. Expensive (£4.50 for a brie and tomato baguette and a smoothie), but the ripest cheese, sweetest tomatoes and freshest bread make it worthwhile.
(Montague St, Tel: (01) 478 8450)

● **Nectar** The Red Spot Launderette is here transformed into a hip juice and smoothie joint and they also have a new branch in Exchequer St.
(53 Ranelagh Village, D6, Tel: (01) 491 0934, Exchequer St, Tel: (01) 672 7501)

● **The Soup Dragon** Soup and Smoothie Heaven!
(168 Capel St, D1,
Tel: (01) 872 3277)

Joose Smoothies:

■ **The Squeeze:** Strawberry, Banana, Orange Juice
■ **The Blend:** Blueberry, Banana, Orange Juice

■ **The Shake:** Raspberry, Banana, Apple Juice
■ **The Twist:** Blueberry, Raspberry, Apple Juice
■ **The Grind:** Raspberry, Strawberry, Apple Juice

Wicklow knowhow

● The **Avoca Handweavers** shops at both of their cafés, in Kilmacanogue and Powerscourt, are superb places to find good foods. A lot of what they sell under the Avoca labels are actually made by some of Ireland's smartest artisans, so the quality is uniformly high with everything, from relishes and oils through to fantastic chocolates, whilst the imported foods are always top-notch. There is a singular aesthetic in the way in which the Avoca team operate that is very noble and pleasing, and the shops and cafés are don't-miss-'em destinations. Look out for local specialities such as Twine Oils, from Ashford, which are particularly beautifully packaged and make great gifts.
(Kilmacanogue, Tel: (01) 286 7466, Fax: 286 2367, Powerscourt House, Enniskerry, Tel: (01) 204 6070 Fax: 204 6072, avoca.ie)

● Jenny Craigie's **Grangecon Foodstore & Café** brings food lovers to this remote little village for tasty traiteur cooking, saving you, to quote them, 'Time, hassle and a messy kitchen'.
(Grangecon, Tel: (045) 403982)

● Another great shopping experience can be had at **Murtagh's**, in the pretty village of Enniskerry. Denise Cray and her team work hard to stock their lovely shop with delectable things, and there are also extremely good cooked foods-to-go.
(The Square, Enniskerry Village, Tel: (01) 276 0404)

Great Irish foods to find in the supermarkets:
IDAS SMOKED TROUT

BOUNTEOUS BIO-DYN

■ You may not be the sort of person given to walking around farms, but if you found the time to stroll around Penny and Udo Lange's **Ballinroan Bio-Dynamic Farm** whenever they hold one of their open days, you'd want to be careful, for you could easily find that the tour of the farm could have the most profound effect on you. Quite simply, Ballinroan Farm is a farm as farms should be. It is a complete entity unto itself, a mixed farm with crops and livestock, and it is home to the most superb vegetables and salad leaves and other foods that you have ever seen. We know people whose entire focus on food has been altered by this visionary couple, artisans who express the artist implicit in the word artisan better than anyone else. You may reckon bio-dynamics is a load of mumbo-jumbo: if so, come and visit here, and you will eat your words, for the proof of bio-dyn is here shown to be profound in every way. Mrs Lange sells her produce at the Dublin Food Co-Op, and through a box delivery system. (Kiltegan, Tel: (0508) 73278, Fax: 73424)

■ Another inspirational Wicklow grower is **Marc Michel**, of Kilpedder, who now has a farm shop open at the farm on Thursdays, Fridays and Saturdays. Mr Michel has always had an unorthodox and very dynamic concept of selling his produce, which is sold under the Organic Life label (you can also find it at the Cow's Lane market in Dublin) and the farm shop is another great opportunity to get produce at its absolute peak; no air miles here, not even road miles! (Kilpedder, Tel (01) 281 0545)

Market!

THE BROOK LODGE INN SUNDAY MARKET
The Doyle brothers and Freda Wolfe have established what is unquestionably Ireland's most visionary food and accommodation venture in the thunderously fine Brook Lodge Inn, and as part of the complex of shops and the pub which are on the hotel's campus they also hold a Sunday organic market, where producers come and sell their wares in front of the shops. It's a don't miss it! way to spend Sunday afternoon in the heart of Wicklow. (Macreddin Village, Tel: (0402) 36444, Fax: 36580, brooklodge.com)

The South East – Wicklow

● The **Wicklow Wine Company**

Ben Mason and Michael Anderson set up this sparkling wine shop just over a year ago, and with solid backgrounds in the wine trade they hit the ground running. A great shop packed with great wines, great service, and a fine range of specialist foods make up a very desirable place indeed.

(Main Street, Wicklow, Tel: (0404) 66767)

● **The Stone Oven**

Arklow's great food lover's destination is Egon Friedrich's lovely bakery and café, long one of the most important craft bakeries in the country. Wholesome sourdoughs and grain and seed breads are all baked with TLC, and you can find them in various Dublin shops as well as from the bakery itself.

(Kingshill, Arklow, Tel: (0402) 39418)

● **Wicklow Waffles**

Helene le Mahieu makes utterly scrummy, syrupy waffles which are quite singular and well worth hunting down in specialist shops and some supermarkets.

(Baltinglass, Tel: (0508) 81999)

COUNTRY MARKETS

• Wicklow has some of the best country markets in the country, and they are a valuable outlet for organic and artisan producers who sell through them.

• You will have to be early to the Golden Ball at Kilternan on Saturday morning, for if you turn up late the queue in front of you will have everything hoovered up before you get a chance. At 11am on Saturday the North Wicklow Country Market takes place in the Scout Den. On Sundays the Roundwood Market kicks off at 3pm.

• To find details of a country market near you, telephone the Irish Country Markets Association, Swanbrook House, Morehampton Rd, D4, Tel: (01) 668 0560.

Great Irish foods to find in the supermarkets:
CLONAKILTY BLACK PUDDING

Wexford inside track

● **Farmer Direct**

This grand Nissen hut, at Marshmeadows on the eastern side of New Ross, is the sort of food venture that does your heart good. Step up into the door, and you are confronted by local foods from local producers being sold to local folk, and everywhere you look there are happy polaroids of happy producers. Jimmy Ryan runs the show with unflappable charm, and don't miss it. (New Ross, Tel: (051) 420816)

Farmer Direct: what we bought...

- Eggs from Catherine Murphy
- St Killian cheeses from Paddy Berridge
- Cakes and bakes and biscuits from Stable Diet
- Paganini ice creams
- Bacon from Laurence Murphy
- Potatoes from Urrin farm
- Apples and apple juice from Ballycross apple farm
- Vegetables from David Rowe and from Iverk
- Kilmurry jams
- Beef and lamb from Brendan Stafford

WEXFORD BERRIES

The sunny south east is home to many producers of soft fruit, so during the summer season make sure to stop at the roadside set-ups which many growers establish to buy superb Wexford strawberries —
the very taste of the south east.

THE WEXFORD CHEESES

The sunshine of the south-east produces fine pastures and gives a marvellously grassy complexity to the local cheeses.

● Perhaps the best known is the **St.Killian** cheese made by Paddy Berridge, sold virtually everywhere in Ireland and very distinguishable on account of its hexagonal box. Let it get a bit mature – ie buy it from a good cheesemonger – and the cheese has a fulsome complexity that belies the fact that the milk is pasteurised.
(Adamstown, Enniscorthy, Tel: (054) 40560)

● There is also a larger-size cheese, **St Brendan Brie**, with a lighter taste, which is also widely available. (Adamstown, Enniscorthy, Tel: (054) 40560)

● One of the cult Irish farmhouse cheeses is Luc and Anne van Kampen's **Mine Gabhar**. A raw goat's milk cheese, they have recently begun to produce it in a log-shape, as well as the traditional round. It is a sensational blast of flavour, beautifully balanced, zinging with herby, sweet flavours. Open your best bottle of claret when Mine Gabhar is on the table.
(Ballynadrishogue, Blackwater, Tel: (053) 27331)

Pettitt's:

We reckon Pettitt's supermarkets are the best small chain of supermarkets in Ireland.
• The shops are brilliantly managed by the family team.

• They sell their own beef from their own farms – and it is superlative.
• They are developing their own bacon factory.

• They support a team of satellite growers who supply them.
• Their wine list is

Wexford – The South East

WEXFORD
● Greenacres

Greenacres is the destination store here, for James and Paula O'Connor run one of the most serious wine shops in the south east. The selection of wines is enormous and includes a delivery service throughout the country. It is also a stop for good food.
(Tel: (053) 22975, greenacres.ie)

● Also in the town, look out for **James Meyler's** in The Bullring for fresh fish. (The Bull Ring, Wexford, Tel: (053) 22239), and **Atlantis** on the pier, also sell fresh fish from their own trawlers.

● There is a Friday **Country Market** in the Bull Ring, starting time 9am.

● **Humble Natural Foods** is a good wholefood shop, on North Main Street. (North Main St, Wexford, Tel: (053) 24624)

● Caribbean Variety Store

The essential stop if you are looking for palm oil, efotete, frozen tilapia fish or pounded yam, though the most popular thing in the shop are the Hair Extensions.
(Fettit's Lane, Wexford)

YOLETOWN
● Stable Diet

Katherine Carroll and Vincent Power's company produces truly excellent cakes and bakes and chutneys and salad dressings. They have become such a success that you can even find their biscuits and flapjacks for sale in garage shops! A range of the cakes are sold in Farmer Direct in New Ross
(Yoletown, Broadway, Tel: (053) 31287 stablediet@eircom.net)

only fab, and each year they have a huge wine fair to support local charities.

• 'We have an emphasis on the "small shop"

mentality,' says Des Pettitt, and it shows. Pettitts are a major force for good food in the south east.

• Main St, Gorey, Tel: (055) 21722, The

Duffry, Enniscorthy, Tel: (054) 36202, St Aidan's Shopping Centre, Wexford, Tel: (053) 24055, Wexford Rd, Arklow, Tel: (0402) 39770, pettitts.ie

Waterford knowledge

County Waterford is home to one of only two sheep's milk cheeses made in Ireland.

● Wolfgang and Agnes Schliebitz make both the superb **Knockalara Cheese**, and a **Knockalara Feta** preserved in oil. Both are utterly distinctive: the original mild and citrussy, slightly crumbly and with a wanly yellow colour, whilst the feta in oil is one of the very best you can buy anywhere, a perfect alliance between the sharply defined flavour of the cheese and the fresh, slightly viscous oil. You will find them in good delis, and they are also used to great effect by local chefs. (Cappoquin, Tel: (024) 96326)

● **Knockanore Farmhouse Cheese** Eamonn Lonergan is one of the great food pioneers of Waterford. His Knockanore cheeses are hard-pressed cheeses, using the milk from their own herd, and are flavoured with herbs and garlic, chives, black pepper, as well as the plain cheese. There is also an oak-smoked version. The cheese really benefits from being matured, when it strikes a perfect alliance of fudgy taste and pleasing texture. The Knockanore cheeses are quite widely available in supermarkets throughout the country. (Ballyneety, Knockanore, Tel: (024) 97275)

● In Cappoquin, you simply have to visit **Barron's Bakery**, where the bread is still hand-made and baked in old stone ovens. Lovely shop, lovely tea rooms also, beautifully run by Joe and Esther Barron. (Cappoquin, Tel: (058) 54045)

● Pick up a pound of good pork sausages at **Michael Murphy's Meat Centre** on the Main Street (Cappoquin, Tel: (058) 54539, and

as you are heading out of town going to Dungarvan, look left and you will see the orchards from which Julia Keane makes the brilliant **Crinnaghtaun Apple juice**. This is one of the great Irish drinks, a true, cloudy, juice which is made from natural juice (and not concentrate) and which is not refined. This means that Crinnaghtaun has the sharpness and balance coming straight from Bramleys and Cox's Orange Pippins. Happily, Crinnaghtaun is widely available, and it is a most brilliant, serious drink.
(Cappoquin, Tel: (056) 54258)

● In Dungarvan, three key addresses: don't miss **John David Power's** excellent butcher's shop, where you will find some of the best bacon you can buy in Ireland. John David Power is just one of the talented people doing their best to resurrect the art of curing great bacon (for others see panel right.)
(Dungarvan, Tel: (058) 42339)

● There is always an excellent range of fish and shellfish at Rose Hickey's **Helvick Seafood**, on Cross Bridge Street, at the L&N car park.
(Dungarvan, Tel: (058) 43585)

BRILLIANT BACON

■ **John David Power**
See left

■ **Gubbeen**
Just try Fingal Ferguson's maple cure

■ **Ummera Smoked Bacon**
The aroma of Ummera frying has everyone's nose perking up. Old style, very salty, very fine.

■ **O'Flynn's Smoked Bacon**
Beautiful bacon from the Cork maestros

■ **Hick's of Sallynoggin**
Excellent green bacon

■ **Rudd's**
Widely available bacon from County Offaly, superb quality

■ **Caherbeg Free Range Pork**
Great old-style bacon

■ **O'Doherty's of Enniskillen**
The black bacon is legendary

■ **Moss-Brook Farm Shoppe**
Trevor sells his fantastic sausages and bacon at the St George's Saturday market in Belfast

■ **Moyallon Bacon**
Jilly Acheson's bacon and meat products from rare breeds are superb

The South East – Waterford

● Still in Dungarvan, Aongus Walsh runs a lovely little wine shop on Friary Street, **Wine World**, an excellent store which shows the owner's sharp vinous discrimination.
(Dungarvan, Tel: (058) 45600)

● In Waterford, the **Gourmet Bakery**, facing the river, is a good choice for some interesting continental-style breads and sweet baking. (Waterford, Tel: (051) 304866.

● A don't miss! address in the city is David Dennison's wonderful **Wine Vault**, on High Street. This is one of the most individualistic wine cellars in the country, and David Dennison not only stocks a fantastic range of wines, he also knows everything about them and has a great delivery service and hamper service to boot. A key address.
(Waterford, Tel: (051) 853444, Fax: 853777, bacchus@eircom.net)

● And whilst in the county do try to track down one of the icon foods: Grichi Gallwey's fantastic **Gallwey's Chocolates**. These wonderful truffles are made in a tiny little factory in the basement of the Gallwey home in Tramore. Grichi Gallwey began to make whiskey truffles back in 1992, then experimented with praline, and most recently has produced coffee truffles. These are utterly individual chocolates, lush, intense, almost decadent. You will find them in the best delis and wine shops throughout the country. (Rockfield House, Tramore, Tel: (051) 381208)

A little local secret:

You can buy desserts to take away in Christine Power's White Horses Restaurant,
(Ardmore, Tel: (024) 94040)
Their Best Selling Desserts Are:

• Tiramisu
• Mississippi Mud Pie
• Banoffi
• Fruit Tart
• Fresh Fruit Meringue Roulade

Smart shopping

Should you suddenly find yourself parachuted into any county in Ireland the most important facts food lovers need to know are:

▪ **Where are my local organic growers and where do they sell?**

All organic growers are members of either the **Organic Trust** or **IOFGA**, the Irish Organic Farmers and Growers Association. The head offices of both organisations can mail or fax a list of local producers, including any who may operate box delivery system. These are the email numbers you need to know:

IOFGA
• (0506) 32563
• iofga@eircom.net

Organic Trust
• (01) 8530271)
• organic@iol.ie
• http://ireland.iol.ie/-organics

▪ **Where are my local markets and country markets?**

Many organic growers also sell through local **Country Markets**, which are vital sources of good food, and through **local markets** which are one of the most dynamic areas of growth for good food right now.

▪ **Where else?**

Hunt down local foods in wholefood shops – again, usually the first port of call for artisan producers – and in SuperValu supermarkets. Many SuperValus are run by enlightened grocer's shops and they encourage local producers.
Then, using this book, you will find the other significant shopkeepers and sources, the leading chocolatiers and cheesemakers, the best wine merchants and wine shops.

Good sourcing is the secret of good shopping.

Sourcing safely:

Butchers shops are usually the best place to buy locally reared meat. Many butchers organisations impose standards high above the norm. For example, in Northern Ireland, look for butchers who are members of the Elite Guild, (elitebutchers.com) and in the south, for butchers who are members of the Associated Craft Butchers of Ireland. (ACBI Tel: (01) 296 1400 acbi@eircom.net). An Bord Bia also applies a Quality Assurance Scheme for Irish beef, pork and lamb.

Louth the inside track

● Peter Thomas' **Bellingham Blue** cheese is the only raw milk blue cheese made in Ireland. The milk comes from the family herd of friesians, and the cheese is matured for six weeks before packaging, being turned by hand each day. It's a semi-hard cheese, and in some ways it is reminiscent of a Stilton, but it's quite definitely a Stilton in overdrive, for with some maturity the cheese has powerful, intense flavours and a richness of taste and texture that is delightful. You will find Bellingham Blue in cheese shops such as Sheridan's of Dublin. (Mansfieldstown, Castlebellingham, Co Louth, Tel (042) 9372343 glydefarm@eircom.net)

● You will find **Cooley Distillery** whiskeys in every multiple and off-licence throughout the country. The whiskeys are produced at Riverstown, and since the first bottles were released in the early 1990's, the range has grown steadily, and now includes the Locke's, Inisowen and Kilbeggan brands, as well as the peated Connemara single malt and the light and very pleasing The Tyrconnell. These are excellent whiskeys and Cooley is valuable as competition to Irish Distillers who otherwise have a monopoly on whiskey production in Ireland.
(Riverstown, Dundalk, Tel: (042) 937 6102)

● **Johnny Morgan's Fish Shop** on Market Street in Dundalk is a proud, busy shop with excellent wet fish.
(7 Eimear Court, Market St, Tel: (042) 27977)

● In Drogheda, **Kieran's Brothers** is a good deli with a number of interesting specialities.
(15 West St, Drogheda, Tel: (041) 983 3728)

The Cavan pioneers

● **Boilie Cheese**

The Brodie family's Boilie cheese is a revolutionary product. It is an artisan product, made by hand, yet it is stocked in every shop in Ireland. Just taste the goat's cheese, preserved in oil, and you will understand why it has triumphed without a jot of compromise: it's a beauty. The cow's milk cheese is milder, and goes marvellously well with smoked salmon and other fish.

(Ryefield Farm, Bailieboro, Tel: (042) 966 6848, info@ryefield.com, ryefield.com)

● **Corleggy Cheese**

Silke Cropp is not just a pioneer cheesemaker, her goat's milk Corleggy and cow's milk Drumlon cheeses valued by food lovers the length and breadth of the country, she is also a pioneer marketeer, for weekends will see her at the Temple Bar, Dublin Food Co-Op and Brook Lodge Inn markets in Dublin and Wicklow. Beautiful cheeses, and do look out for the fresh cheeses.

(Corleggy, Belturbet, Tel: (049) 952 2930, corleggy@eircom.net)

● **Thornhill Duck**

Ken Moffat's duck and geese are peerless. The intensity of flavour with which they reward the cook is a direct result of the care shown by this expert producer in rearing and looking after his stock. Find them in Dublin in Caviston's, Downey's, O'Toole's and McKiernan's.

(Thornhill, Tel: (072) 53044)

Great Irish foods to find in the supermarkets:

No. 1 LAGER

Carlow knowhow

● The **Carlow Craft Brewery** is one of the most outstanding craft brewers in Ireland, and, with **O'Hara's** 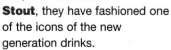 **Stout**, they have fashioned one of the icons of the new generation drinks. O'Hara's is so toasty, hoppy, dark, rich and luscious that it's virtually a shock the first time you taste it. If you are of a certain age, you will remember when other stouts had such persistence and wildness of flavour. The big commercial brews have forsaken idiosyncrasy, so it's down to brewers such as Brendan Flanagan to take up the mantle for beer lovers. The other two brews from the company – the red ale **Molings** and the hoppy lager **Curim** – are both

excellent, but O'Hara's is one of the indispensable tastes of modern Ireland. You will find it in pubs all around County Carlow. (The Goods Store, Station Rd, Tel: (0503) 34356, Fax: 40038, ccb@iol.ie)

● In Carlow town, check out **Bosco's** butcher's shop, on Tullow Street, a model modern butcher's shop which is a Carlow institution, with great foods and great service.
(132 Tullow St, Carlow, Tel: (0503) 31093, Fax: 31498)

● If you drive all the way to Tullow, then check out **Laz Murphy's** butcher's shop, another very highly regarded source for good meat farmed and sold in the traditional way.
(Church St, Tullow, Tel: (0503) 51316)

Great Irish foods to find in the supermarkets:
BALLYMALOE BROWN BREAD MIX

Brilliant brews

BREW PUBS

■ Some of Ireland's craft brewers only sell their brews in their own pubs, so you need to go to the **Franciscan Well** pub in Cork to try their excellent brews. (13b North Mall, Tel: (021) 439 3434, Brewery: (021) 421 0130, franciscanbrewery.com) ■ Whilst in Dublin you have to visit both **The Porterhouse**, (16 Parliament St, D2, Tel: (01) 679 8847) and **Messrs Maguire**, (Burgh Quay, Tel: (01) 670 5777 Fax: 6705500, messrsmaguire.ie) as their brews are draught only. ■ In Thurles, you need to check out the stylish **Dwan's Brew pub**, just down from the main square. Don't worry, though: you'll find such visitations aren't too much of a hardship. (Thurles Tel: (0504) 26007, dwan.ie)

CRAFT BREWERIES

■ The brews which you will find in wine shops and off-licences include the **Carlow Brewing Company's** brilliant trio, also the excellent **No.1 Brew,** brewed in Kildare, which is actually in many supermarkets. (The Goods Store, Station Rd, Tel: (0503) 34356, Fax: 40038, carlowbrewing.com) ■ The **Biddy Early** brews, from County Clare, are increasingly widely distributed – look out for **Red** and **Black Biddy**. (Inagh, Tel: (065) 36742 beb.ie) ■ You will also be able to find the quartet of brews from the **Celtic Brewing Co** of County Meath. (Enfield, Tel: (0405) 41558) ■ The fantastic beers of the **Dublin Brewing Co** can be found in good wine shops in Dublin and abroad, and none of these should be missed: the **Maeve's Crystal Wheat** is an astonishing drink, the other three brews from the company almost as exciting as this liquid icon. (Nth King St, D7, Tel: (01) 8728622, dublinbrewing.com) ■ In Northern Ireland, look out for the fine Hilden beers from the **Hilden Brewing Co** (Hilden House, Grand Street, Lisburn, Tel: (028) 9266 3863) and be adventurous and try to track down the brews of the **Whitewater Brewery** (40 Tullyframe Rd, Kilkeel, Co Down, Tel: (028) 4372 6370) ■ The **Kinsale Brewing Co** makes Ireland's newest brew. (Lander's Brewery)

Kildare inside track

● Food lovers are pie lovers, and no one makes a better pie than **Mary Morrin**, who bakes for her local country market in **Naas** on Friday mornings, and has also established a little farm shop, at her house just outside **Kilcock**. If you love fine crumbly pastry surrounding enticing fillings, then this is a place of pilgrimage on Fridays, when the shop is open from 3-8pm. There isn't a weak link in Mary's work, and she is blessed with having her own butter and milk to work with, along with their own beef and vegetables: fab steak and kidney pies with a hot water pastry; sweet lamb scented with cumin; sublime pear and Roquefort pie; excellent salmon with dill and fennel, the ever-popular chicken and ham; the terrific apple and Stilton tarte tatin. Pie Heaven.
(Kilcock, Tel: (01) 628 4411)

● In **Naas**, Susan and Valerie continue to expand both their range of foods and wines in **Cuisine de Vendange**, a sweet little shop just opposite the church off the main strip of the town. They also now offer Butler's Pantry prepared foods, as well as Tipperary organic ice cream, and lots of good wines.
(1 Sallins Rd, Naas, Tel: (045) 881793, srouine@eircom.net)

● There are more excellent wines in **The Mill Wine Cellar** in **Maynooth**, a small shop packed to the roof with good things to drink.
(Mill St, Maynooth, Tel: (01) 629 1022)

Great Irish foods to find in the supermarkets:
BALLYBRADO BISCUITS

Kilkenny knowledge

Kilkenny is Ireland's craft centre, and the county offers craft lovers the chance to embark on a seriously good tour of talented craftspeople.

● But food lovers aren't neglected either, so start with Olivia Goodwillie's fantastic **Lavistown Cheese**, made on the farm a few miles outside the city. The cheese is pale white, and somewhat in the style of a Caerphilly. It has a delightful crumbly cleanness and a buttermilky sharpness. Best of all, as a true artisan cheese it is delightfully variable throughout the year: no two Lavistowns are ever quite the same. There is no other cheese like Lavistown.

Olivia also makes some of the most distinctive **sausages** you will find, cylinders of the purest pork with delicate seasoning. You will find these for sale locally in Shortis Wong, in The Gourmet Store, and they feature on the menu in The Design Centre and in Café Sol. And, don't overlook the excellent courses which the Goodwillies run at Lavistown, everything from flower painting to mushroom hunts. (Lavistown, Tel: (056) 65145, courses@lavistown.ie, lavistown.ie)

ORGANIC BOX DELIVERY

Perhaps it was an idea ahead of its time, but the surge of interest in box delivery systems has not proven to be the ideal producer to consumer solution people imagined a couple of years ago.

Nevertheless, some of the very best Irish growers from Donegal to Wicklow to Kerry do continue to distribute their own food in the locality, to appreciative food lovers. Source details from IOFGA and the

Organic Trust if you wish to get involved in a weekly box delivery scheme.
IOFGA
• (0506) 32563
• iofga@eircom.net
ORGANIC TRUST
• (01) 853 0271)
• organic@iol.ie

Kilkenny – The Midlands

PILTOWN

● Eilis Gough's **Mileeven** company is the powerhouse of hand-made foods in Kilkenny. Their preserves are as appreciated as their excellent cakes, and old-style cakes such as whiskey cake and fruit cake are purest delights. Whatever they produce is distinguished by exceptionally high standards, which explains how this dynamic company's foods are distributed so widely.
(Owning Hill, Piltown, Tel: (051) 643368)

KILKENNY

● In Kilkenny city, the vital address for shopping is **Shortis Wong**, one of the finest delis-cum-ethnic shops you will find. Mary Shortis and Chris Wong really understand their foods, and they are great enthusiasts, as well as great cooks and bakers. Don't miss it.
(74 John St, Tel: (056) 61305)

● And do hunt down the **Gourmet Store**, on High Street, where Padraig and Eileen Lawlor sell excellent sandwiches and food to go, along with local specialities. (56 High St, Tel: (056) 71727)

● Another good stop, for sausage lovers, is **Kieran White's** butcher's shop, on Parliament Street.
(4-5 Parliament St, Tel: (056) 63248)

Best selling home-made 'Street food' from Shortis Wong:

■ Spring rolls
■ Samosas
■ Fried noodles
■ Fried rice
■ Spicy wedges
■ Quiche

'All the above are made with different fillings, but we find all things without meat are going better. We'll make anything to order.'

Laois inside track

I COULDN'T LIVE WITHOUT:

'Sally Barnes' Woodcock smoked fish, the products from the West Cork Herb Farm, as well as Janet Drew's relishes, and all the Irish cheeses, particularly those made locally by Pat Hyland.' JIM TYNAN

● Gee whiz, but Helen Gee is the girl of the moment in Laois. Mrs Gee's fantastic **Gee's Jams** are the great local success story of Portlaoise, and when you get a taste of these pure, fruit-driven jars of goodness you will understand why. Top quality fruit, simple preparation in open pans and lots of TLC make for some of the best jams and marmalades you can buy. (Abbeyleix, Tel: (0502) 31058)

● You will find G's jams in **Jim Tynan's The Kitchen**, in the centre of Portlaoise, and whatever you do, don't miss this shop: in fact, detour off the motorway into town to shop and eat here. The Kitchen is one of the great Irish shops, and Jim Tynan is one of the most important figures in Irish food. Everything he can get his hands on that is good will be for sale here, along with fantastic baking which simply can't be beaten. (Hynds Sq, Portlaoise, Tel: (0502) 62061)

● And what you will find here is Laois's own cheese, Pat Hyland's creamy, mild, organic **Abbey Blue Brie**. As well as the conventional brie and blue cheeses, there is also a good smoked version, and look out for their organic St Canice sheep's milk cheese. (Cuffsborough, Ballacolla, Tel: (0502) 58559)

Great Irish foods to find in the supermarkets:
LIR CHOCOLATES

Longford truffles

● What is a model small Irish food company like? Somewhat like Ruth McGarry-Quinn's **Torc Truffles**, we reckon. A small factory to make the delectable chocolates and truffles, a fabulous shop and café in the centre of Longford from which to sell them, and about 20 happy people employed in this gleaming, smart operation, with everything bearing the bubbly, stylish signature of the chocolatier herself. Fantastic.
(Longford, Tel: (043) 48277)

HELLO SWEETIE

The following are some of the leading Irish sweetie specialists:

- **AINÉ** Very stylish, very hip chocs from Dublin's Ann Rudden
- **BIZZY LIZZY** Lovely continental-style sweet things from Tipperary
- **BUTLERS CHOCOLATES** The Butler's operation now also has chocolate cafés in Dublin city
- **O'CONNAILL** Casey O'Connaill is one of the longest-established chocolatiers
- **CHEZ EMILY** Darling chocs from Helena Hemeryck
- **CHOCCA MOCCA** Geoff Caird and Catherine Melvin make really witty, fun sweeties
- **DRUID CHOCOLATES** Lush creamy chocs from Gareth Vaughan, and check out that groovy website: www.druidchocolate.ie
- **FLAIR CONFECTIONERY** Eve St Leger is the great chocolatier of Cork city; we'll have the crunchy bars please
- **GALLWEYS OF WATERFORD** Grichi Gallwey's super-rich truffles are unique, seriously good and a serious indulgence
- **LIR CHOCOLATES** Conny Doodie's firm are pioneer chocolatiers: don't miss the Bailey's truffles
- **SKELLIGS CHOCOLATE CO** It is worth going all the way to Ballinskelligs to visit this story-book factory. Amazing chocs, amazing packaging
- **WILDES CHOCOLATES** Delightfully handsome chocs from County Clare

Meath inside track

ASHBOURNE

● What we love about Claire Mooney's **Baking House** breads is the fact that Ms Mooney has thought of everything. 'This cellophane bag can be added to your compost', it says on the label, so these breads are as ecological as it gets. Everything is organic, and the loaves are excellent, and actually get better after a day or two, not that they last that long! Look out for the pain de campagne, made with San Francisco sourdough culture. You will find them in The Dublin Food Co-Op on Pearse Street on Saturday morning.
(Harlockstown, Ashbourne, Co Meath, Tel: (01) 835 9010)

● Of the many outstanding relishes made and sold in Ireland, the one that disappears fastest in our house is **Janet's Country Fayre's** sweet pepper relish, an awesomely irresistible food. You may be unaware of it simply because Ms Drew makes her relishes to be sold under shop labels – so in the Gallic Kitchen they are Gallic Kitchen relishes, in Manning's Emporium they are Manning's Emporium relishes, and so on. They are quite amazingly good: contact Janet for details of the individual stockists.
(Janet's Country Fayre, The Garden Cottage, Ballinlough Castle, Clonmellon, Tel: (046) 33344, Fax: (046) 33331)

● **The Celtic Brewing Co.** is a small, bespoke brewery which grew out of a beer distribution company run by Dean McGuinness. Their principal brews are **Finian's Irish Red Ale** and **Finian's Gold**, and this pair have been joined by both a stout and a lager. The brews are pasteurised, and all are good, and you will find

them in good wine shops and off licences.
(Enfield, Tel: (0405) 41558)

NAVAN

● **The Ryan Vine** is a smart wine shop beside the Ryan Family's Bar on Trimgate Street, with an excellent range of wines,

also good Riedel glasses, and a wine club with monthly tastings.
(22 Trimgate Street, Navan, Tel: (046) 78333)

● Another fine wine shop is Elaine Teehan's **The Noble Rot**.
(Navan, Tel: (046) 73489)

Mother's Milk: Irish Brews & Irish Cheeses

Get into the groove with your friends and match Irish farmhouse cheeses with artisan brews for a true treat. The following, which we 'worked on' with Kevin Sheridan for a presentation at the Slow Food Salone del Gusto, are merely suggestions: feel free to disagree!

- Ardrahan with O'Hara's Stout
- Smoked Gubbeen with 1798 Revolution Ale
- Cooleeney Camembert with d'Arcy's Dublin Stout
- Mine Gabhar with Hilden Ale
- Durrus with Molings Ale
- Coolea with An Dubhain
- Bellingham Blue with No1 Brew
- Cashel Blue with Maeve's Crystal Wheat
- Gabriel & Desmond with Beckett's Gold
- St Tola with Porterhouse Oyster Stout
- Milleens with Rich Ruby Country Ale
- Corleggy with Finian's Original Gold

Great Irish foods to find in the supermarkets:
IRISH GOLD VENISON

Offaly: the inside track

● The ones to grab first are the rhubarb-flavoured yogurt and the strawberry-flavoured yogurt. Whatever else they may do with their milk – and they sell it in cartons, as well as making plain and low-fat organic yogurts and excellent kiddy-yogurts – the Cleary brothers have managed with their **Glenisk Fruit Yogurts** to produce two of the most delicious foods you can eat today in Ireland. There are no fewer than nine Cleary brothers, all involved in the business, all working out of the old Tullamore Dairies which was established by their father. Their visionary venture just goes from strength to strength, making them vital pioneers in bringing organics into the mainstream, where it belongs, where it works to raise standards and create an alternative consciousness. And, of course, to create pleasure, the sheer pleasure which these conscientiously produced, visionary foods give us.
(Killeigh, Tullamore, Tel: (0506) 44259)

RUDD'S BACON

Andrew Rudd is one of the second-generation artisans working in Ireland whose youthful energies have given ever-greater dynamism to a model family food company. Rudd's bacon and sausages were first produced by dad David and mum Pru, before the younger generation took over. Now operating out of a state-of-the-art factory, Rudd's produce superb pork products, which have their own idiosyncrasies – the sausages and puddings are quite unlike anything else produced today – and yet which manage to work successfully in the mainstream.
Their widespread distribution is the triumph of good taste over bottom-line economics.
(Busherstown House, Moneygall, Tel: (0505) 45206)

Great Irish **cookbooks**

■ **The Avoca Café Cookbook**
Superb food from the inspirational Avoca team.

■ **The Ballymaloe Cookbook**
by Myrtle Allen. An ageless classic, full of profound wisdom.

■ **The Café Paradiso Cookbook**
by Denis Cotter. Quite simply the finest cookery book ever written by a practising chef. A classic.

■ **The Cork Cookbook**
Now quite rare, but worth hunting down for this great collection of recipes from County Cork's finest cooks.

■ **The Drimcong Food Affair**
by Gerard Galvin. Perhaps the wisest book ever written on the practice of being a restaurateur.

■ **Hot Food**
by Paul & Jeanne Rankin. A forgotten title from Belfast's dynamic couple, and unquestionably their masterpiece.

■ **Irish Traditional Cooking**
by Darina Allen. Scores of marvellously rustic and agrestic recipes.

■ **Land of Milk and Honey**
by Brid Mahon. Pioneering study of Irish culinary history.

■ **A Little History of Irish Food**
by Regina Sexton. Engaging writing and lively wit from Cork's food-loving scholar.

■ **Pizza Defined**
by Bernadette O'Shea. The text of the brilliance of Ireland's most iconoclastic cook.

■ **The Potato Year**
by Lucy Madden. 365 potato recipes described with great felicity.

■ **You Say Potato**
by Elgy Gillespie. The most rollicking recipe book ever on Irish food.

Tipperary big county

VISIONARIES AND CHEESEMAKERS

Peter Ward is the greatest grocer in Ireland and his shop, Country Choice on Kenyon Street in Nenagh, is testament to what a good local shop, in the hands of a gifted shopkeeper and cook, can achieve and amount to as part of a town and part of a culinary community.

Peter Ward and his wife, Mary, understand the detail and the depth of detail that is needed to make something special. Others sell farmhouse cheese: Mr Ward matures it until he is happy that it is ready, and then he sells it, understanding every nuance of every cheese he works with. He bakes the most sublime hams, terrines, pâtés and roasts you can make. His breads are fabulous, and the marmalade Peter and Mary make every year, using Seville oranges, is an icon food in its own right.

He is a master of sourcing specialist foods of the highest quality from Ireland and abroad. He has a terrific selection of wines. His Christmas hampers are peerless. His staff are charming and, as if all that wasn't enough, Mr Ward also runs a delightful café at the rere of the shop, where the cooking is only ace.

What explains this ability to be the best? Empathy, we reckon. Empathy for the hard work of the artisans whose foods he sells. Empathy for the traditions of Irish food which he keeps alive with his soda bread, his brawn, his other traditional foods. And empathy with his community, his understanding of their true needs, and his ability to satisfy them, in the most appropriate – and charming – way.

This is shopkeeping raised to the highest art form, with the shopkeeper as shaman, sage, chef and connoisseur. Country Choice: was there ever a place so well named?

(25 Kenyon St, Nenagh, Tel: (067) 32596, countrychoice.ie)

Tipperary

● The other visionary food producer of the county is Josef Finke, of **Ballybrado**. Mr Finke is one of organics most committed and eloquent advocates, and also responsible, via his Good Herdsmen and Ballybrado companies, for getting organic meat to a large audience via supermarkets. He also manufactures the fine range of Ballybrado biscuits. Aside from this, his on-going advocacy of organics has been of vital importance in bringing the government and the public around to appreciating small-scale, high-quality food production.
(Cahir, Tel: (052) 66206)

●**Tipperary Organic Ice Cream** is another new and visionary venture. Run by Paddy and Joyce O'Keeffe, TOICs have scrummy flavours: chocolate and hazelnut; banana and cinnamon; hazel amaretto macaroon. Very exciting, very yum yum.
(Carrigeen, Clonmel, Tel: (052) 81905)

BEEF COUNTRY

● Tipperary beef is as fine as it gets, and if you buy beef from the fine butchers of **Nenagh** – **Michael Hackett** on Connolly Street (Tel: (067) 31340) and

CHEESE COUNTRY

The lush pastures of Tipp make for great milk, and the county has some of the most successful and distinguished cheesemakers in Ireland.

■ **The Maher family now have two generations involved in making the sublime Cooleeney Camembert, on the family farm at Moyne, near to Thurles. This oh-so-delicate cheese has a fist of flavours in a velvet glove texture. Dreamy, runny and lush, the cheese reveals tangy mushroom and woodland flavours. This is one of the greatest Irish cheeses, but you need to get it from a good cheesemaker to see the cheese perform at its brilliant best. The family also make the popular Dunbarra cheeses, good everyday semi-soft cheese in various flavours which can be found in every supermarket.**

■ **Another family with a pair of cheeses are Jane and Louis Grubb, who make the**

Gregory and **Michael Hanlon** on Kenyon Street (Tel: (067) 41299) – then you get Tipp meat where the vital conjoining of good herdsmanship, small-scale and sophisticated slaughtering, and excellent butchering skills are brought together. In **Urlingford,** the model practice of **Bergin's** butchers once again produces meticulously fine beef. Just try this, and you will understand what the locals rave about. (Urlingford, Tel: (056) 31660/31119) And smart locals with freezers buy organic beef from **Michael Hickey**, of **Gortrua**, one of the longest established organic farmers in Ireland. Michael breeds his own stock, from a pedigree Angus bull, and the animals are slaughtered locally and sold direct to customers. (Tel: (062) 72223)

APPLE COUNTRY

● Tipperary is also apple country and, as with cheese and beef, the apples here get transformed, by the best people, into something superlative.

The leading exponent of superb apple juice is Con Traas, of the (imaginatively titled) **The Apple Farm**, on the road between Cahir and Clonmel. Here is how you make a superb apple juice. First of

CHEESE COUNTRY

brilliant Cashel Blue cheese, and who have been winning new plaudits for their startlingly fine Crozier Blue, a sheep's milk blue cheese which is only fabulous.

The secret of Cashel Blue, aside from remarkable consistency in the cheesemaking over the last 15 years, is the fact that it needs ageing: 10 weeks old will do, but 12 weeks is even better, for then the flavours have sufficient time to balance and blend. The Crozier Blue, likewise, needs time for all the flavour elements to come together, but when they do, boy! this is a stunner.

■ **Baylough is a beautifully made cheese which uses the finest milk. Dick and Anne Keating profit from this superb milk, for it bestows Baylough with a fudgy-sweet flavour. Some of the cheeses are flavoured, and there is also a smoked cheese, but we reckon the mature plain Baylough is the cream of the crop.**

all, you harvest by hand, so that the sugar content is as high as 16% (in normal apples, 9% is standard). You choose varieties carefully, so that the characteristics of the blend are distinctive, so Mr Traas uses the unusual Karmijn, along with Bramley's Seedling. The Karmijn performs well in Ireland's climate, as well as having the aroma characteristics of a tree-ripened Cox's Orange Pippin, and thus features hundreds of esters and other volatiles. You then pulp the apples, press the pulp in a rack and cloth press, collect and bottle the juice and pasteurise in bottle to prevent fermentation. And when you have done all this, what do you get? A drink worthy of the Gods, is what. This is an incredibly fine apple juice. The best fun is to take a trip to the (imaginatively entitled) The Apple Farm, to buy from the man himself, though they are becoming more widely distributed as time goes on. (Moorstown, Cahir, Tel: (052) 41459, signposted on N24 between Cahir and Clonmel)

OTHER FAB APPLE JUICES

■ **BARNHILL APPLE JUICE**
Made by Kenneth Redmond near Portadown, we like this served very cool, when the effervescent bouquet is shown at its best.

■ **CRINNAGHTAUN**
Fantastic juice from Julia Keane of Cappoquin. Amazing freshness and balance make this a super serious drink. Widely available.

■ **CUMWIN'S APPLE JUICE**
Cumwin's is hard to find, but it's a fine apple juice, pressed on the farm near Dungannon, delivered and sold locally.

■ **THE LITTLE IRISH APPLE Co**
A dry, fresh juice made with Bramleys and seasonal dessert apples near to Piltown in Kilkenny.

■ **LLEWELLYN'S IRISH APPLE JUICE**
Look out for David Llewellyn's Dublin-produced apple juice in wholefood shops, a very refreshing, cool drink, and do try to get a taster of his cider at the Temple Bar Market.

 Great Irish foods to find in the supermarkets:
DUNN'S SMOKED SALMON

Westmeath knowhow

ATHLONE

● A bounteous store with great food and wine is Alan Algeo's **Al Vinos**. There are 500 different wines for sale here, along with a very carefully selected selection of Irish and continental cheese. Alan is a true enthusiast for great wines and great foods, so ask for advice about special bottles. (Irishtown, Tel: (0902) 74589 alvinos@indigo.ie)

● In the town, do check out the excellent range of cookware in **Burgess'** department store, on Church Street. Rosie Boles and her team have a super-discriminating selection of vital things for the kitchen. (Tel: (0902) 72005 info@burgessofathlone.ie)

CORBETSTOWN

● In Corbetstown, Anne Holtown makes the precious **Corbetstown Goats Cheese**, using milk from Jill and Ray Oliver's herd, and whilst this is a relatively new cheese, it has already won a silver medal in the British cheese awards. It's a semi-hard cheese, pleasantly vanilla sweet when young, and even better aged for about six months when the sweetness becomes more profuse.
(Corbetstown, Killucan, Tel: (044) 74845)

MULLINGAR

● Sheena Shanley and Bernard Smyth initially established **Cana Wines** to import their favourite wines from Italy, which they then distributed to restaurants and hotels. Late in 1999 they opened their smart **Cana Wine & Food Store** on Castle Street, and ever since it has been a place to wander into and linger longtime, absorbed by the provocative foods and wines they stock. Whilst the Italian section is strong, given that they import directly from several producers, they sell wines from all over the vinous world, and excellent deli foods from cheeses to coffees. There are tastings in-store on Saturdays.
(10 Castle Street, Tel: (044) 42742)

Westmeath – The Midlands

● Paddy Keogh doesn't just love wine, he loves the whole world and culture of wine. He loves discovering something new, and then tracking the winemakers down in their vineyards, wherever that may be, from France to California. He loves writing about the new wines in his newsletters, he loves introducing the wines to his customers, he loves selling the wines to restaurateurs. And this enthusiasm is infectious: somehow a case of **Wines Direct** wines coming through the post always feels like a treat, rather than just another order of vital daily drinking to maintain one's equilibrium. There isn't a dud bottle on his list, but some special bottles such as the outstanding l'Hortus range from SW France should not be missed, and for the sort of scintillating quaffer that he seems to find in the back of beyond, just try the Domaine St Hilaire, again from SW France. Great wines, excellent site, fantastic speedy service through the mail.

(Irishtown, Mullingar,¡ Tel: 1800-579579, wines-direct.com
sales@wines-direct.com)

Tormey's Butchers:

What you need with some of the best Wines Direct red wines is the best Westmeath beef, for they are serious about their meat here, and none more so than James Tormey's butcher's shop in Mullingar, where many folk argue that the beef is the very best you can buy in Ireland. To enjoy the magnificent taste and texture of this beef is a treat, but don't overlook all the other good things in this state-of-the-art butcher's shop: such artistry with meat is sensational. Harbour Centre, Tel: (044) 45433, also Galway Shopping Centre and Tullamore.

Great Irish foods to find in the supermarkets:
CASHEL BLUE FARMHOUSE CHEESE

Donegal: archetypes

Dibbles and Filligans sounds like a dubious solicitor's firm, or perhaps a team of feng shui consultants. In reality, Dibbles and Filligans are two of the most remarkable small food companies in Ireland.

● **Dibbles** is run by Roisin Jenkins, and is as far north in Donegal as you can get. (Port na Blagh, Tel: (074) 36655, roisin@dibbles.ie, dibbles.ie) **Filligans** is run by Philip and Sarah Moss. (Glenties, Tel: (075) 51628, moss@ gofree.indigo.ie) Both companies produce the most scintillating preserves, with Dibbles concentrating on savoury relishes and dressings, whilst Filligans also produce excellent jams and marmalades along with relishes. Both companies' foods have signature style, fab flavours, and true originality.

And, remarkably, both small companies send their foods out from the wilderness to the metropolitan centres: you will find Dibbles in all the supermarket chains, you will find Filligans under various labels, including its own, in places like Avoca Handweavers and in smart Gourmet Ireland hampers. But what is equally important as the benchmark quality is that they work and create employment right at the periphery, where conventional wisdom says that such things cannot work. But, taste these foods just once, and you will want them again and again. These are prototype companies, indeed, let's call them archetype food producers for the future.

Great Irish foods to find in the supermarkets:
GLENISK RHUBARB YOGURT

Donegal – The North West

● In Donegal, contact the **North West Organic Producers' Group (NWOPG)** a cross-border grouping of organic producers who publish a regular newsletter and who have details of how to source their produce. (Copley, Muff, Tel: (077) 84107 nwopg@eircom.net)

● A superb bio-dynamic producer who supplies his produce via a local box system is **Thomas Becht** of Glenties, and do look out for his speciality products; contact Thomas for details. (Dorian, Glenties, Tel: (075) 51286)

● You will find local foods, including produce from the Organic Centre in Leitrim, in **Simple Simon**, on The Diamond in Donegal, which is a truly vital wholefood shop, with some fine breads, excellent cheeses, Filligan's preserves, local yogurts, all the good things. (Anderson's Yard, The Diamond, Tel: (073) 22687)

● In Letterkenny, there are interesting wines for sale in **De Vine Wines** on Pearse Road, including a host of excellent bottles sourced from Searson's of Monkstown (Pearse Rd, Tel: (074) 71730)

Foods to find in local shops

- Macnally Farm Yogurt
- Bonina Black pudding
- On the Wild Side Tapenade of sea vegetables
- Fish out of Water smoked oysters
- Hederman smoked mussels
- Carraig Fhada sea vegetables
- Oisin Farmhouse Cheese
- Killaloe Delicatessen meats
- Con Traas apple juice
- Sabores de Mexico jalapenos
- Carraig goat's cheese
- Ummera smoked chicken
- Poulcoin cheese
- Aillwee Charcoal
- Moyallon wild boar
- Dorian Farmhouse Cheese
- Goya's Chocolate Gateau

Leitrim: mavericks

ROSSINVER

● The mavericks favour Leitrim. Rod Alston came here and started **Eden Plants** decades ago, and today it is one of the great icons of organics in Ireland, a source of the most perfect herbs you can buy, home to some of the most pristine organic vegetables you will ever enjoy, which can be found in shops such as the **Co-Op Shop** in Manorhamilton, and in Tir na nOg in Sligo. If you have the chance, then do visit the farm, for it is an inspiration.
(Rossinver, Tel: (072) 54122)

● Mr Alston was also instrumental in setting up **The Organic Centre**, at Sraud, where John O'Neill is now the manager and Klaus Laitenberger the head gardener. Here be more mavericks, more visionaries, for the centre exists to educate the public via its courses, and to supply local households via its box delivery system. Again, a visit, and especially taking one of their courses, is inspirational.
(Rossinver, Tel: (072) 54338, theorganiccentre.ie)

CARRICK-ON-SHANNON

● Down in Carrick-on-Shannon, Trevor Irvine did a very maverick thing in establishing **Cheese Etc** in the town, for who would have thought a specialist cheese shop would prosper in a small town. But prosper it has, and Mr Irvine now also masterminds Caís Cairdiúil, the **Irish Fine Cheese and Wine Society**, established with Cavan cheesemaker Silke Cropp. They have offers, organise dinners, and any food lover in the region really should be part of this maverick little group.
(Bridge St, Carrick-on-Shannon, Tel: (078) 22121)

New Irish brands

brand **consciousness**

Shoppers and supermarkets are nowadays fixated on the concept of brands, products whose identity is instantly recognisable and whose quality represents an understood compact with the consumer. Successful artisan brands include Cashel Blue, Darina Allen Ice Cream, Boilie, Glenisk, Gubbeen Cheese and Clonakilty Black Pudding. Here are some new ones to watch.

- AYA Sushi
- Ballymaloe Relish
- Barry's Earl Grey Tea
- Benoskee Cheese
- Bubble Bros
- Bunalun 160 Organics
- Caherbeg Pork
- Corbetstown Cheese
- Crozier Blue Cheese
- Dibbles Preserves
- Good Herdsmen
- Gubbeen Bacon
- Irish Yogurts

- Java Republic Coffee
- Kinvara Sm'kd Salmon
- Maeve's Crystal Wheat
- Mrs Collins' Ice Cream
- Noodle House Pasta
- O'Hara's Stout
- Riverville Cheese
- Rudd's Bacon
- Sabores de Mexico
- Skelligs Chocolate Co
- Stable Diet
- Tipperary Ice Cream
- West Cork Herb Farm

Sligo: food route

Sligo has little reputation as a place to eat, but it is a very good town in which to shop for wonderful foods. Here is where you should go. Just follow the arrows (in the text!) to make a perfect food lover's tour of this beautiful Western town.

⇨ **CASTLE STREET**

Kate's Kitchen is the icon address in Sligo, for Kate Pettit's shop just gets bigger and better and, since the move to Castle Street, Kate's gets busier and busier. Everything that is good in the region makes its way here, and is sold by Kate and Frank with great grace and knowledge. This is an unmissable address when in Sligo for every manner of specialist food and for good food-to-go.
(3 Castle St, Tel/Fax: (071) 43022, kateskitchen@eircom.net)

● And don't miss checking out two interesting shops on either side of Kate's: **Cat & Moon** (Tel: (071) 43686) and **Cross Sections**, (Tel: (071) 42265) for lots of covetable things for the house, whilst for modern furniture, head to Rockwood Parade, to **Space**, Gráinne Dunne and Brian Raftery's precious outlet for modern furniture in the North West. (Tel: (071) 28877)

Great Irish foods to find in the supermarkets:

IRISH YOGURTS CRÈME FRAÎCHE

Sligo – The North West

⇨ GRATTAN STREET

Mary McDonnell, is one of the great revolutionaries of
Irish food. For two decades she has stocked the foods
of the best local producers and thereby supported
them and helped them survive and prosper. Today, she
remains as critical and polemical about the food
business as ever, and **Tir na nOg** remains home to great
foods, sold with selfless conviction by Mary.
(Grattan St, Tel: (071) 62752)

● **Octavius** Michael Gramsch runs one of the quirkiest
wine shops you can find, and it is a happy home to
many bottles which you simply won't find anywhere
else, like good quaffers from Gramsch's home region of
the Pfalz to mega-buck blow-out bottles such as
Domaine de la Romanée Conti. This is a beaut of a shop and
should not be missed by wine lovers. (Grattan St, Tel: (071) 71730
octaviusfinewines@oceanfree.net)

⇨ MARKET STREET

Ah, **Cosgroves**! A grocer's shop just as they used to be,
with shelves stocked high and handsome with good
things to eat, a real old-fashioned counter across which
you order, and true, gentlemanly service. Part of the
fabric of the town, and the council should place a

Great Irish foods to find in the supermarkets:
BARRY'S EARL GREY TEA

preservation order on it pronto for this is as vital a part of Sligo's culture as Hargadon's pub. If Ridley Scott walked in here, he'd be back shooting a Hovis commercial in the morning. Nostalgia is never lovelier than this.
(32 Market St, Tel: (071) 42809)

● **Bar Bazaar** A funky coffee shop run by Richard and Tamasin Cavallero, home to the splendiferous Illy coffee.
(Market St, Tel: (071) 44749)

⇨ **BRIDGE STREET**

The Gourmet Parlour is one of the key Sligo addresses, home for more than a decade to the sort of inspired, modest home baking which makes your heart as glad as your tum. Annette Burke and Catherine Farrell have great sandwiches at lunchtime, vital foods to go for dinner, and their savoury and sweet baking is fantastic. Excellent party and catering service also.
(Bridge St, Tel: (071) 44671.

GREAT SLIGO FOODS

■ **NOODLE HOUSE PASTA**
**Ingrid Basler's Noodle House Pasta is one of the vital modern convenience foods.
Meticulously made, and a godsend for good fast food for kids, it is one of the best realised artisan foods in Ireland. The use of impeccable ingredients and drying at low temperatures means this is a true handmade pasta. It is widely available.
(Curry, Tel: (071) 85589)**

■ **CARRAIG FHADA SEAWEED**
**Having conquered the world of sea vegetables with his unimpeachably fine selection of dried seaweeds, Frank Melvin has boldly moved into the leisure market with the launch of his Carraig Fhada Seaweed Bath. This lubricious little bag of seaweed goodness transforms your tub into a sexy seaweed sensation. There is nothing else like it, and it is just as innovative and imaginative as all of Mr Melvin's seaweed products. You'll find them in wholefood stores.
(Rathlee, Tel: (096) 49042)**

Clare the inside track

County Clare foods have an intense regionality, which means not only that they are blessed with the natural flavours of the West Coast, but also that many of them, in fact, never travel much beyond the borders of the county.

CHEESE

● **Poulcoin Cheese** is made by Anneliese Bartelink, and you will find it in some of the county's wholefood shops, as well as some markets around the country. Ms Bartelink was one of the pioneer cheesemakers in Ireland, and her utterly correct gouda-style cheeses are superb, and of particular note because they are so expertly flavoured, with garlic, cumin and nettles. Hunt high and low for these. (Telephone number withheld, and the cheese is not available from the farm. Hunt it down in local shops and B&Bs)

● Other West Coast cheese secrets include Paul Keane's **Bluebell Falls Goat's Cheese**, now packed in neat little tubs which make it much more accessible than before. This is a subtle, pleasing, fresh goat's cheese, and you will find it in delis and wholefood shops from Clare to Connemara, but nowhere else. (Ballynacally, Tel: (065) 683 8024)

Great Irish foods to find in the supermarkets:
DARINA ALLEN ICE CREAM

The West – Clare

● **Kilshanny Cheese** is another local secret, again found in shops in Clare and also at the Saturday Limerick market. This is a fine gouda-style cheese, strongly-flavoured when mature, or if you buy some of the flavoured cheeses. Amanda Nibbering and Dick de Valk, the cheesemakers, also run a B&B at their home in Derry House, which you will see signposted on the road north of Lahinch.
(Lahinch, Tel: (065) 707 1228)

● The one farmhouse cheese which has made its way – and created its reputation – beyond the borders of the county is **St Tola**, now made by John McDonald, a delightful engineer-turned-cheesemaker, who continues the great tradition of goat's cheese making begun almost 25 years ago by Meg and Derrick Gordon.
The cheese is sold as the traditional fresh, soft goat's cheese and also in a mature,

hard form when it is sold at about 6 weeks old. Do search for the little crottins they make also, and note that you can follow the signs for the St Tola farm which you will see on the road between Inagh and Ennistymon, and buy some cheese from the cheese-making factory itself. John and his team also sell the cheese at local markets such as Ennis on Sunday, Kilkee on Saturday and Ennistymon on Tuesday.
(Inagh, Tel: (065) 683 6633, saint.tola@iol.ie)

● Another well-known farmhouse cheese is Sean and Deirdre Fitzgerald's **Cratloe Hills Sheep's Cheese**. Aside from the rarity of sheep's milk cheeses in Ireland, this is notable for the fact that the small, mature orbs of cheese are exceedingly good. Like St Tola, Cratloe Hills cheeses are widely available.
(Cratloe, Tel: (061) 357185)

● Don't forget to track down the **Burren Gold** cheeses of the **Aillwee Caves**, aged gouda-style cheese with different flavours, and a new Feta cheese in olive oil
(see page 81 for more details.)

Clare – The West

SMOKED FOODS

● Whilst you can order Peter Curtin's superb smoked fish through the internet, there is still nothing nicer than turning up at the **Burren Smokehouse** in Lisdoonvarna to buy his wonderful smoked mackerel and the relatively new smoked organic salmon. This is a place of pilgrimage for food lovers, and the overall consistency and style of Mr Curtin's fish is only brilliant.
(Lisdoonvarna, Tel: (065) 7074432, Fax: 707 4303, burrensmokehouse.ie, sales@burrensmokehouse.ie)

PRESERVES

● In the best shops in Clare you will find David and Vera Muir's fine **Clare Jam Company** jams, and these are expert, fruit-driven jams worthy of anyone's breakfast table.
(Lough North, Doolin, Tel: (065) 707 4778, Fax: 707 4871 clarejam@eircom.net)

CRAFT BEER

● And Clare is lucky to have one other great treat. Just at the crossroads in

CHARCUTERIE

■ So, take a trip down to Miltown Malbay, and search in the local butchers' shops for Teresa de Barra's Bonina Black Pudding. This is sold in a cake-tin shape (a little like a tea loaf) and it is a delightful pudding, quite unlike any other, with a subtle, lingering flavour of cinnamon and allspice making it a true, barley-filled treat. Local restaurants and B&B's serve the pudding, and you can buy it in the butcher's shops in Miltown Malbay, in Haughs and Fitzpatricks in Ennistymon and in Jordans in Lisdoonvarna. (Miltown Malbay, Tel: (065) 84156)

■ Equally expert are the salamis, cured meats, kabanossi and sausages produced by the Killaloe Delicatessen, in Killaloe. It is quite incredible that these special foods are not better known and don't travel beyond Clare, because they are terrific, so don't miss them. You'll find them in most of the SuperValu shops in Co Clare, as well as the specialist shops. (Killaloe, Tel: (061) 923069)

Inagh, the **Biddy Early Brew Pub** is run by Niall Garvey. This was the first pub and artisan brewery in Ireland, and production is still done in extremely small batches. There is a little visitors' centre at the brewery, but the real delight here is in tasting the excellent Black Biddy and its sisters, Red Biddy and Blonde Biddy. These are unique beers, which use age-old ingredients such as carrageen moss and bog myrtle for fining the beers and to add body. They are not to be missed, and can also be found in various other outlets in Clare and Limerick. (Inagh, Tel: (065) 683 6742, info@beb.ie, beb.ie)

● There are three reasons to go to the **Aillwee Cave**, just outside Ballyvaughan. One is to do the tour of the caves, which is fab. The second is to search for Ben Johnson's splendid **Burren Gold** cheese – get some of this when it is well-aged and you get a truly expert, satisfying, mustardy-mellow cheese, and don't miss his new feta cheeses. The other thing to pile into the car is the Aillwee Charcoal, environmentally coppiced hazel which is unequivocally the best charcoal you can buy in Ireland. Once you try this, you will never use a commercial barbecue fuel again. (Ballyvaughan, Tel: (065) 7077036, Fax: 7077107, aillweecave.ie)

CHARCOAL

Most of us pick up our bags of charcoal from petrol station forecourts and, truthfully speaking, we shouldn't. The charcoal is usually of dire quality, 98% of it is imported, it comes from tropical and mangrove swamps and is extracted with little provision for regeneration. All good reasons to avoid the forecourt stuff.

Aillwee Caves charcoal, on the other hand, is made from coppiced hazel woods, where the trees are cut in strict rotation, then allowed to grow again for a number of years. This style of coppicing has been practised in Ireland for 6,000 years, and such a system means that broadleafed trees will regenerate. The fuel is pure, and has no additives. It burns like a dream and, best of all, it cooks your barbecue food perfectly: manageable heat which is ready in 10-15 minutes, with delicious smoky, woody aromas that bless the food with flavour. A fantastic fuel, as vital for a barbecue as cold beer.

Clare – The West

If County Clare has great produce, it also has some great shops, which do their very best to promote what is local and what is special about the county.

BALLYVAUGHAN

● In Ballyvaughan, you will find the best foods of the county in Sheila McGannon's **Village Stores**, a smart Spar shop just at the edge of the village.
(Ballyvaughan,
Tel: (065) 7077181
villagestores@eircom.net)

ENNIS

● In Ennis, the vital shop is Anne Leyden's excellent Ennis **Gourmet Store**, where you can find absolutely everything good which the county has to offer, as well as some fine wines Anne and David Lasblaye, her partner, import direct from France. The shop is also notable as being one of the great hamper producers in Ireland, and Anne will make true bespoke hampers for any customer, including a Clare hamper which features most of the county's best foods.
(1 Barrack St, Tel: (065) 684 3314, gourmetstore@eircom.net)

● Also in Ennis, you need to know that the locals get all their catering for special occasions done by TJ McGuinness and Brenda Deering in **The Food Emporium**, on Francis Street, just across from the Poor Clare's Convent.
The consistency and quality of Mr McGuinness's work hasn't dimmed a jot over the many years we have known him, and this is also a great spot for lunch and for good coffee.
(Francis St, Tel: (065) 682 0554)

Great Irish foods to find in the supermarkets:
GOOD HERDSMAN ORGANIC LAMB

● Another vital address in Ennis is **Open Sesame**, a greatly-expanded wholefood shop which sells many of the county's artisan foods along with organic fruit and vegetables and wholefood essentials. Look for the fresh goat's milk, and enquire here about organic box delivery systems. (29 Parnell St, Tel: (065) 682 1480)

ENNISTYMON

● We just love **Unglert's Bakery**, a little bread and cake shop in Ennistymon. The bearded and patient Mr Unglert is a fine baker, the sweet things are yummy and squishy and delicious, and how wonderful that the tradition of the local village bakery manages to survive here. (Ennistymon, Tel: (065) 707 1217)

LISCANNOR

● If you want to buy specialist wine in County Clare, then there is no happier trip than the journey to **Patrick Egan's Pub** in Liscannor. Egan's is a beautiful pub, but it is the range of classed-growth clarets which Mr Egan sells, along with some more-affordable wines from little chateaux and some Spanish specialities, which makes this a happy, indeed unique, vinous pilgrimage.
(Liscannor, Tel: (065) 7081784/7081430)

THREE FAVOURITE GOURMET STORE HAMPERS

■ THE CLARE HAMPER
Filled with local foods from throughout Co Clare, including all the Clare cheeses, Bunratty mead, Clare Jam Co jams & chutneys, Lisdoonvarna smoked salmon, Kilalloe salami and smoked ham, Tuamgraney champagne truffles.

■ THE GOURMET HAMPER
Estate olive oil, aged balsamic vinegar, porcini mushrooms, sun-dried tomatoes, olives, smoked ham, smoked salmon, salami, chutneys, pasta sauces from Lime and Lemongrass, spices and herbs.

■ THE CORPORATE HAMPER
– Vintage Port, Sauternes, French vintage wines, champagne tuffles, smoked salmon, cheeses, including Stilton, Irish cheeses, crackers, panettone, after dinner mints, Irish biscuit selection.

Galway: inside track

GREAT GALWAY SHOPS

• • • • • • • • • • • • • • • •

● Goya's

Emer Murray's boutique bakery is the best in Ireland, a
spiffing combination of extraordinary sweet baking,
fantastic breads and fruit cakes, and a darling room in
which to buy them from. Ms Murray makes baking as
chic and cutting-edge as food style can get, and Goya's is
one of the most vital food lover's destinations in the country. (Kirwan's
Lane, Tel: (091) 567010)

● Sheridans Cheesemongers

Galway's Gourmet Grand Central, is how local writer
Aran McMahon has described Sheridan's
Cheesemongers, and it's an utterly apt slogan for this
dynamic, irrepressible team. Now in a fine new
premises on Castle Street, which allows them more
room for making lunchtime food, and to display vegetables
and herbs, they remain the most vital address in town for the very
best artisan cheeses and foods. Do look out for the new things that
make their way here: last time we were in it was a new cheddar-style
cheese being made by an Australian lady somewhere in County Clare.
Unmissable.
(Castle Street, Tel: (091) 564829)

Great Irish foods to find in the supermarkets:
KINVARNA ORGANIC SMOKED HAM

McCambridges

This genteel old grocery and wine shop feels like a step-back in time in today's world of frenetic retailing.
Gentlemanly service, excellent foods and a good wine counter, a calm ambience, means McCambridge's has no need to change with the times, for they do things right today, just as they have always done.
(Shop St, Tel: (091) 562259)

McDonagh's

A fish and chip shop and a fish restaurant, with an affiliated wine bar across the street, McDonagh's is a power on Quay Street. They also actually sell the wet fish which has made the restaurant's reputation throughout the years.
(Quay St, Tel: (091) 565001)

C.R. Tormey & Sons

This butcher's shop in the Galway Shopping Centre on Headford Road is one of the three shops owned by the Tormey family, with the beef for the shop coming direct from their own farm in the Midlands. It is of impeccable provenance and as good as it gets, but then everything else is just as meticulously prepared in this state-of-the-art shop.
(Galway S.C. Tel: (091) 564067)

SCRUMPTIOUSNESS

Emer Murray's best selling cakes at Goya's are:

■ **CHOCOLATE GATEAU**
Sponge, soaked in orange Cointreau, filled with white and milk chocolate mousse, painted with dark chocolate icing.

■ **CRANBERRY AND ALMOND TART**
Pastry case, almond frangipane, fresh cranberries, flaked almonds. The cranberries burst into the frangipane.

■ **APPLE AND RASPBERRY JONATHAN**
Apples, raspberries, and the topping is a cross between a shortbread and a Madeira.

■ **ORANGE MADEIRA CAKE**
Classic Madeira, flavoured with orange juice and orange zest, available miniature and full-sized. Split in half and filled with white chocolate butter cream.

■ **FRUIT SCONES**
Shortbread scones, with raisins, and granulated sugar – to give texture.

Galway – The West

WINE & CHEESE

● **The Noble Vine** Noel O'Loughlen is not just wine seller, but also vineyard owner and winemaker these days, with vineyards in SW France. His nose for a good bottle, an idiosyncratic bottle, is as sharp as ever, and it makes The Noble Vine a must visit address for wine lovers. (Terryland, Galway, Tel: (091) 565749 noblevine@eircom.net)

● **The Vineyard** Muriel Kineen's shop on Mainguard Street in the centre of the city has an excellent range of wines, well chosen, with a bias towards the Old World dictated by the preference of her customers. (Mainguard Street, Tel: (091) 561816)

● **Riverville Farmhouse Cheese** Robbie and Anne Gannon's gouda-style cheese is one of the artisan newcomers. Using milk from their own herd, there are a range of flavoured cheeses in addition to the plain and smoked cheeses. Two silver medals at the British Cheese Awards were well deserved. (Craughwell, Tel: (091) 848232)

Smoking Permitted:

• **Kinvara Smoked Salmon** Declan Droney's mildly-flavoured smoked salmon is of organic standard, with the fish reared close to Clare Island off the West Coast. Its mildness and delicate texture explain its considerable success, and this is a food to search for. (Kinvara,

Co Galway Tel: (091) 637489 organicsmokedsalmon. com)

• Three other smokehouses to look out for are the smoked salmon from the Aran Islands, the lovely smoked products such as smoked eel from Old Village Smokehouse, and Graham Robert's smoked fish from Connemara.

• **Aran Salmon**,

(Kilronan, Inis Mor, Aran, Tel: (099) 61240, aransalmon@eircom.net

• **Old Village Smokehouse** (Douras, Woodford, Tel: (0509) 49064)

• **Connemara Smokehouse** (Bunowen Pier, Aillebrack, Ballyconneely, Tel: (095) 23739, Fax: 23001, johnroberts@ smokehouse.ie www.smokehouse.ie)

CONNEMARA

■ **Flemings Fish Delivery**
Gay and Freda Fleming operate a fish delivery service around Galway, selling fresh fish. The fish is prepared as the customer orders it, skinned, boned, portioned etc, and then vac packed and quickly frozen. Telephone to place an order.
The Old Coastguard Station, Rossaveel, Tel: (091) 572088)

■ **McGeough's**
Eamonn and James McGeough's meat tastes like no other. Their lamb and beef are amazing – herbaceous, sweet, pure, a dream to cook with. Their experiments – such as James' recent splendid attempts at an air-cured ham – are inspiring, and they are a charming father-and-son team. Honestly, there is nowhere nicer to buy meat in the whole country, simple as that. And, if you buy Connemara lamb here, you will know that it is true Connemara lamb, sold only in season. (Lake Road, Oughterard, Co Galway, Tel: (091) 552351)

■ **The Connemara Hamper**
Eileen and Leo Halliday are discriminating folk, and you need only look at the bounteous, choice foods they stock in the invaluable Connemara Hamper, in the centre of Clifden, to appreciate just how much they know, and how much they care, about artisan and speciality foods.
This is one of the very best delis, and if you are renting a house in Clifden during the season, this is your first stop to stock up, and last stop to take goodies back home. (Market Street, Clifden, Tel; (095) 21054 abaco@iol.ie)

Great Irish foods to find in the supermarkets:
RUDD'S BACON

The Galway **market**

It is likely that the Saturday morning Galway market, arranged in a wrap of streets around the Collegiate Church of St Nicholas, smack in the centre of the city, may well come to be regarded as the most significant statement on behalf of good food in Ireland.

For a start, it was created by the people who come here to sell, and supported by the people who come here to shop, and both these groups have persevered and prospered despite the attempts of officialdom to make their lives as awkward as possible.

The success of the venture, with local people buying local foods from local producers, has been both prototype and archetype for the markets that have followed throughout Ireland, all of them in some way or other imitative of what happens here every Saturday morning. The Galway market broke the mould of genteel country markets and created an institution where organic foods were given as a base line, where hand-made methods were the very thing that attracted the punters, and where true craic and bonhommie offered a vital alternative to the sterility of a supermarket shopping experience.

For these reasons, the Galway producers broke the mould, and today Cait Curran, Dirk Flaake, Willem den Heyer, the Sheridan brothers, Moyglass Bakery, Brekish Dairy and all the others who turn up to trade here every week offer one of the icon experiences of Ireland.

 Great Irish foods to find in the supermarkets:
BOILIE GOAT'S CHEESE

Limerick knowhow

Market!

There are a few destination stalls to hunt down in and around the Limerick Saturday market.

● Inside the Milk Market, head straight for Marie Murphy's **Greenacres** stall, where you will find the ripest, most perfect cheeses sold in the city, all sold with enviable panache and wit by Marie. She is particularly good at having cheeses ready for Saturday which beg to be taken straight home and scoffed, lovely Irish and Continental cheese in oozing, lush magnificence. Cleverly, shoppers always get to taste the cheeses, which inevitably results in overflowing shopping baskets. Her imported bread is good too. During the week deli goods are for sale in the shop, which overlooks the market.
(Tel: (061) 400334)

OISIN FARMHOUSE CHEESE

Rose and Rochus van der Vaard, makers of the various cheeses which come under the Oisin Farmhouse Cheese stable, work against the grain of conventional artisan cheesemaking. One day in a shop you might find something by them which is close to a cheddar, made with cow's milk. From a market stall you might buy a pale white goat's cheese, with the most scintillating taste and droolsome consistency. Next time it might be a blue cheese you find. They are pioneers, experimenters, and thrilling cheesemakers, so whatever it is you find for sale, simply buy it: their skill guarantees it will be thrilling, an improvisation composed with milk.
(Kilmallock, Tel: (063) 91528)

Limerick – The West

● Outside the market, look for Olivier Beaujouan's **On the Wild Side** stall. Though based in Tralee, M. Beaujouan is one of the great regulars of the market, and his foods are simply amazing. Recently, he picked up three medals at the Great Taste Awards for his unique creations: silver medal for pickled kombu; silver for his tapenade of sea vegetables; and a bronze for his tartare of kombu. There is nothing else like these made or sold by anyone else and do check out his excellent fish products as well, which are just as funky.
(Tel: (066) 718 0194
seatoland@hotmail.com)

● You will find lots of farm fresh eggs, domestic baking and good local vegetables in the market, and some organic growers also sell from stalls on the outside, so hunt these down. There is also a stall from the Alternative Bread Co, and a stall selling County Clare's Kilshanny Farmhouse Cheese.

● **The Wild Onion,** is a taste of Chicago brought to the market quarter. All day American-style food is served in the café, and for the shopper, their home made breads and US cakes and cookies can be bought to take away.
(High St, Cornmarket, Tel: (061) 440055, wildonioncafe.com)

LIMERICK CITY

In the centre of Limerick city, look out for smoked bacon and the local speciality, Packet, from **Maher's Bacon Shop** on Parnell Street (Tel: (061 416653), discover Asian specialities in **The Oriental Food Store** on Roches Street (Tel: (061) 417139), head to **John Sadlier's** shop just down the hill on Roches Street for fresh fish and poultry (Tel: (061) 414232). And for wine, you can choose between Terry McCann's **Speciality Wine Shop** on Denmark Street (Tel: (061) 412445) or one of the branches of **Fine Wines,** where the main shop is on Roches Street (Tel: (061) 416501), with lots of other branches dotted throughout the city, from Castletroy to Dooradoyle. One of the key Limerick addresses has long been **Rene Cusack's** fine big fish shop down on Dock Road, close to the bridge, a real professional operation with fine fish (Tel: (061) 317566), whilst the leading deli is just outside the city: at Caherdavin, **Ivan's** is a super-smart, stylish shop packed with good things chosen with care by Ivan Cremins. (Tel: (061) 455766)

Mayo: market

Market!

● The best of the local foods in County Mayo bring themselves to the frenetic **Westport Thursday Market** at the Town Hall, and you need to be here early if you want to get the best local cheeses, fresh organic herbs and vegetables, excellent domestic baking and jams and pickles. In the summertime especially, when Westport's population triples with holidaymakers, getting out of bed early on Thursday is a must. The Thursday market is one of the delights of the West, packed with varying foods and producers depending on just who has got just what and what time of year it is. Don't miss it.

● Two butchers from the county deserve special mention: **Ryan's Butcher's** shop in Cong (Tel: (092) 45059) and **Kelly's Butcher's** shop in Newport (Tel: (098) 41149) are two benchmark family country butchers which also supply excellent family restaurants which adjoin the shops: **Echoes** in Cong and **Kelly's Kitchen** in Newport. Both shops sell superb meat, and Kelly's also make simply fabulous sausages, so banger lovers mustn't miss this.

● Susan Kellet's **Enniscoe House**, near Ballina, has seen massive improvements to their gardens recently, and one of the practical benefits is the box delivery scheme of organic vegetables which Michael Gara organises.
(Tel: (096) 31003)

Great Irish foods to find in the supermarkets:
WEST CORK HERB FARM SAGE JELLY

Cork good food county

EAST CORK

Midleton Saturday Market **What you need to know**

Kate O'Donovan will be grilling the sausages she has brought from **O'Flynn's** in Cork and will be selling her fine **Marble Hall Marinades.** The **Ballymaloe** stall always has lots of interesting vegetables from their gardens, as well as fine eggs, and even free-range ducks from time to time: in summertime look for tomatillos and other rarities. There are good breads from Marog O'Brien's **Farmgate** shop and restaurant, frozen prepared organic beef from **Dan Aherne**, matured **Ardsallagh** cheeses made by Jane Murphy and what you have to look for in particular are the mustard and black pepper cheeses which Jane only sells in the market, and there will be lots of other **farmhouse cheeses** sold at her stall by Fiona; there will be **Hederman smoked fish, Willy Scannell's Ballycotton potatoes** (get there early or these will be sold out), **Glenribben Organics** from West Waterford, and lots of other interesting producers. Mighty fun, and not to be missed.

We bought:

- **Three-year-old Ardsallagh and smoked Ardsallagh**
- **Oisin goat's farmhouse cheese**
- **Ballycotton potatoes**
- **Glenribben Swiss chard**
- **Hederman smoked eel**
- **Ballymaloe brown bread mix**
- **Gubbeen hot bacon roll with Ballymaloe jalapeno relish**
- **Grilled O'Flynn's sausage with Marble Hall relish**

The South West – Cork

Great hard stuff Outstanding Irish Whiskeys

• **Black Bush** is one of the great blended whiskeys, with superb balance amongst all the malty, peaty, sherry goings-on that you will find when you raise the glass.

• **Bushmills 16-year-old Single Malt** The 10-year-old single malt is good, but this is in another league altogether, a profoundly beautiful glass of whiskey.

• **Connemara** The waft of peat off this Cooley Distillery single malt is profound, but the balance and poise of the whiskey is darling.

• **Green Spot** Hard to find (it's sold only by Mitchell's of Dublin and annual production is only 6,000 bottles) and worth the search for this wonderful, dainty, pot still character.

• **Jameson 1780** Most of the whiskeys used in 1780 are actually older than the 12 years it states, and the mature, regal assurance of this great drink speaks of patient distilling and care.

• **Power's Gold Label** For our money one of the greatest drinks in the world. A classic that one simply can never tire of.

• **Redbreast 12 year old** Originally known as "The Priest's Bottle", and you can always trust the clergy to know a good hootch when they drink it. Tremendous pot still characteristics make for the sexiest whiskey of them all.

• **The Tyrconnell** From Cooley Distillery, this single malt has a light, citrussy style, not unlike a Scottish single malt, and it's terribly easy to drink!

SHOPPING IN MIDLETON

■ **The Farmgate** is a legendary Cork institution, with an excellent small bakery and lots of good foods in the shop attached to the café.
(Midleton,
Tel: (021) 463 2771)

■ Jill Bell's **Well & Good** is one of the most discriminating wholefood shops – come here for rarities such as Traas apple juice, organic vegetables from local east Cork growers, and also to get details of meetings of the **Cork Free Choice Group**, a vital group of devoted food-loving agit-proppers.
(Broderick St,
Tel: (021) 463 3499)

■ On the main street in Midleton, **Ballycotton Seafood** is a vital stop for fresh fish from Dick Coffey-Walsh and his crew.
(46 Main St,
Tel: (021) 461 3122)

Cork – The South West

SHANAGARRY

● The Ballymaloe empire embraces many different aspects these days, but one of the pivotal elements is Wendy Whelan's **Ballymaloe Shop**, in the grounds of Ballymaloe House. The Ballymaloe shop is one of the very best kitchen equipment shops in Ireland, with lots of covetable cookware and crockery, a small range of very discriminating foods including the various Ballymaloe foods and relishes made by Jasmin Hyde and some lovely olive oils from the Oil Merchant, interesting things for the table and the kitchen – and don't miss the jams made in the Ballymaloe kitchens and especially the speciality Imokilly cheddar which is matured for Ballymaloe House and which you will only find here!
(Ballymaloe House, Shanagarry, Tel: (021) 465 2032)

● In nearby Cloyne, do visit Mr **Cuddigan's Butcher's** shop, in the centre of the village: once upon a time all butcher's shops were like this, once upon a time the meat sold by local butchers was all as good as this. It's a true tonic to come here, and even better to buy the beef and lamb and revel in their astonishing herbaceousness.
(Cloyne, Tel: (021) 465 2521)

● The other must-visit stop is **Stephen Pearce's** emporium in Shanagarry, with masses of covetable, tactile and luxurious crockery in his trademark clay and black colours.
(Shanagarry, Tel: (021) 464 6807)

 Great Irish foods to find in the supermarkets:
MOY PARK ORGANIC CHICKEN

Cookery Schools in Ireland

Cookery Schools

• **Ballymaloe Cookery School**
A great mix of 12-week certificate courses along with guest chefs, gardening courses and many others. Without doubt, the pre-eminent school of cookery in Ireland. (Shanagarry, Co Cork, Tel: (021) 464 6785, info@cookingisfun.ie, cookingisfun.ie)

• **Berry Lodge**
Rita Meade specialises in bespoke classes for small groups, in her house which is also a restaurant and B&B (Miltown Malbay, Co Clare, Tel: (065) 708 7022, berrylodge.com)

• **Ghan House**
Guest chefs are a major attraction in Joyce Carroll's well-regarded school, and Carlingford is a darling place to visit. (Carlingford, Co Louth, Tel: (042) 937 3682, ghanhouse.com)

• **Otto's Creative Cuisine**
Weekend courses by the inspired Mr Kunze, using the finest ingredients from his tunnels. Beautiful location, outstanding teaching. (Dunworley, Co Cork, Tel: (023) 40461 ottos-creative-catering.com)

• **Pangur Ban**
John Walsh opened the school just over two years ago. Fusion cooking has been the big hit, but they will happily teach anything, right from the proper way to boil an egg to goat's cheese wontons with green ratatouille. (Letterfrack, Co Galway, Tel: (095) 41243 pangurban.com)

• **Valentia Cookery**
Linda Booth's classes showcase both her own skills as well as those of very popular guest chefs. Young Neven Maguire (did you see him on the telly!?) is back time after time to wow! everyone. (25 Avoca Park, Blackrock, Co Dublin, Tel: (01) 278 2365)

CHEF'S KITCHENS

A number of chefs now open their kitchens off season for cookery classes.

■ **THE COMMONS**
Aiden Byrne is one of the most exciting talents in Dublin right now, so do get details of these specialist classes, appositely followed by lunch. (85 St Stephen's Green, D2, Tel: (01) 478 0530 thecommonsrestaurant.ie)

■ **ISLAND COTTAGE**
Intense, exciting classes for a pair of learners at a time from the brilliant John Desmond. Unique location on an island off the coast. (Heir Island, Co Cork, Tel: (028) 38102, islandcottage.com)

■ **LONGUEVILLE HOUSE**
For our money, William O'Callaghan is the great unknown genius of Irish cooking, and his classes give the chance to see a truly original talent at work. Anyhow, you deserve a few days in Longueville, don't you? Ah, you do. (Mallow, Co Cork. Tel: (022) 47156 longuevillehouse.ie)

North Cork

North Cork has rich, diverse, ancient pastures, and so it has terrific milk.

●To taste this milk at its best, hunt down some of the milk and butter made by the **North Cork Co-Op**, from Kanturk, and sold as Kanturk milk. The milk is creamy and dreamy, the butter is full-tasting and rich.
(Kanturk, Tel: (029) 50003)

● Then, to see what this milk can be transformed into, just try the two great North Cork farmhouse cheeses.

Ardrahan Farmhouse Cheese, made by Mary Burns on the family farm near to Kanturk, is one of the greatest of Irish cheeses, an intensely flavoured semi-soft cheese with an almost physical assault of herby, mustardy, spicy flavours that seem to linger for ever. Best of all, just pair this with a bottle of O'Hara's Irish stout, and you have Flavour Heaven. Their smoked cheese is also excellent.
(Kanturk, Tel: (029) 78099)

● Young Dick Willems makes the superb **Coolea Farmhouse Cheese** using the summer pasture milk from their dairy herd. At six months old, the sweetness has just begun to express itself, at fifteen months the sweetness of this gouda-

---

Local Secrets:

■ A well-kept secret, of North Cork is Donal Creedon's astonishing Macroom Oatmeal. An astonishing porridge?! Too right. There is no other porridge sold which is anything like this, its slightly smoky, toasty taste and its slightly coarse texture are unique. Donal uses the traditional way of roasting oats. Macroom Flour is also special, and both are available throughout Cork.
(Macroom, Tel: (026) 41800)

style cheese is magnificent, and shows perhaps the longest aftertaste of any farmhouse cheese. Coolea shows great cheesemaking skills and great milk in magnificent alliance. (Macroom, Tel: (026) 45204)

● Visitors to Cork should seek out Nan O'Donovan's sweet, mild **Round Tower** cheese, many local supermarkets stock it. It's a friendly, accessible cheese and always enjoyable. (Enniskeane, Tel: (023) 47105)

● Don't miss Mary and Pat **O'Callaghan's** deli in Mitchelstown, not merely an excellent café for daytime cooking, but also a great source of home-made foods, especially at Xmas: ask about their "secret" sauce for plum puddings. (Mitchelstown, Tel: (025) 24657)

● Just outside Mitchelstown, Michael **Horgan's Delicatessen** supplies has long been a vital distribution nerve centre for the best Irish artisan foods. (Mitchelstown, Tel: (025) 84023)

● In busy Ballincollig, Michael **O'Crualaoi's Butchers'** is a phenomenon. Sometimes, the queue in here for the cooked meals is so enormous you wonder if anyone in Ballincollig ever cooks dinner any more? Or do they just let Michael do it for them? The cooked foods are very good indeed, but it is the fantastic quality of the meats which we admire even more, especially the excellent sausages; don't-miss-'em. (Ballincollig, Tel: (021) 487 1205)

■ **Assolas Preserves are another secret. Hazel and Joe Bourke run one of Ireland's greatest country houses in Assolas, and the sublime skilfulness which** Mrs Bourke brings to her work in the kitchen is found also in their jams, marmalades, chutneys and pickles. You can buy them from the house, order them in the Assolas hampers, and buy them from Lucey's fine butcher's shop in Mallow. (Kanturk, Tel: (029) 50015, assolas.com)

Cork English Market

The mother of all Irish markets is an absorbing cornucopia of the most delicious ancient and modern foods. Tradition and innovation exist side by side here: the pig's tail beside the San Francisco sourdough loaf; the basil pesto with the buttered egg; the organic bak choi with the east Cork spuds; the corned beef with the terrine de la campagne; the gravadlax with the salted ling; the cured bacon bodice with the bottles of bubbly.

It is this ability to nurture the new and protect the old that makes the English Market so utterly vital. Our culinary heritage is disappearing all around us, yet walk into this fine old market and tradition confidently holds its head alongside the fashionable. For this reason, the English Market is the most vital address in Irish food.

What We Bought:

- **A sandwich from Toby Simmond's new sandwich stall**

- **Buttered eggs from Moynihans**

- **Pasta and Parmesan from Iago**

- **Squid and Haddock from O'Connells**

- **Kikkoman's soy sauce and some fresh lemon grass from Mr Bell**

- **Olives stuffed with Anchovies from the Real Olive Co**

- **Five grapefruit for a Euro**

- **Pheasant from Bresnan's**

- **Drisheen from Stephen O'Reilly**

- **Pâté and Arbutus Wholemeal Sourdough from On the Pig's Back**

- **A cup of coffee from Mary Rose Daly's Café Central**

- **Lunch in The Farmgate Café**

- **A sheepskin rug from Willie Beechinor (only joking, Ed)**

Alternative Bread Co.

Sheila Fitzpatrick's ABC bread can nowadays even be found as far afield as the Saturday Limerick market, but the English Market remains their base. Lots of varieties of good bread, including a highly regarded chocolate and prune bread. (Tel: (021) 489 7877, alternativebread.ie)

Mr Bell's

Mr Bell is, in fact, Mr Driss Belmajdoub, and his pair of stalls in the market are a godsend for anyone hunting down speciality ethnic foods. Everything you could imagine and everything you could covet for ethnic cookery is sold here, and then some more. Try to get Mr Bell to give you his recipe for Irish stew, Moroccan-style. (Tel: (021) 488 5333)

Bresnan's

Michael Bresnan's traditional butcher's stall has herbaceous beef and lamb from their own farms, and all the old curing and spicing techniques are still used here to make fantastic, arcane specialities. (Tel: (021) 427 1119)

Bubble Brothers

Billy Forrester's company began as champagne specialists, but have quickly expanded their business to include a complete range of fantastic wines. South West France is the specialist area, along with champagne, but there is real discrimination explaining every bottle Billy Forrester sells. This is, in every way, a model bespoke wine merchant, right from their prompt and polite and helpful service through to an excellent web site. (Tel/Fax: (021) 455 2252, bubblebrothers.com)

I A G O

Sean Calder-Pott's handsome stall is meticulous and very special. The pristine quality of everything Sean and his team make and sell at Iago is inspiring, the attention paid to every detail verging on the obsessive, despite Mr Calder-Pott's laid back calm!
Their fresh pasta is the best you can buy; hunt here for superb mozzarella; for the long-aged Parmesan (unmissable); the basil pesto; the speciality tuna and anchovies, everything. A sheer joy, nothing less.
(Tel: (021) 427 7047)

Cork – The South West

Hederman's Smoked Fish:

Frank Hederman's stall sells the complete range of his
smoked foods, which come in from his smokehouse in
Belvelly, near to Cobh, and sampling them all simply
confirms that here is a masterly epicurean, a fish smoker of
the most consummate skill. Of course the smoked salmon is fantastic,
but it is the other items which showcase this master smoker's signature:
the smoked mackerel which is unlike any other, the smoked mussels
which are simply unique, the brilliant smoked eel. This is as cutting-edge
and cosmopolitan as Irish artisan food gets.
(Tel: (021) 481 1089, Fax: 481 4323)

● The Garden

This lovely stall, on the left as you
come in from Prince's Street, is
dedicated to pristine organic
vegetables, as well as dried nuts and
fruits and some imported specialities.
It is manned by Grace Maher, who is
charming and knowledgeable and
very helpful, as you try to make up
your mind what it is you want. Hell,
you want the lot. (Tel: (021) 427 2368)

● Stephen Landon

Stephen's stall is where
you will get bodice, one
of the market's treats
which are virtually
impossible to get outside of Cork
city, along with a splendid array of
bacon products, and just watch the
way in which this man can tie up a
piece of bacon with string: dazzling!
(Tel: (086) 226 6320)

● On the Pig's Back

Isabelle Sheridan's stall
just gets bigger and
better. It has always
been invaluable for
imported French speciality meats
and salamis, and especially for their
own sausages and pâtés, which are
made using fantastic free-range pork
sourced from Seamus Hogan of
North Cork and which are of superb
quality. The stall is also noteable for
European and Irish farmhouse
cheeses which they bring to
superlative condition. The Pig's Back
is especially vital also for the
outstanding Arbutus Lodge breads,
made by Declan Ryan, which you will
find here from mid-morning: these
are perhaps the best breads being
baked in Ireland right now, so it's
another don't-miss-it reason to get
On The Pig's Back. (Tel: (021) 427 9232)

O'CONNELL'S FISH STALL

Pat and Paul **O'Connell's** fish stall is not just the best fish counter in Ireland, it's also the biggest and the most beautiful, following a spiffing recent refurbishment which has created the most svelte, aquatic sea-blue tiled selling space imaginable. This is as handsome as a cruise ship, but the food product here is a zillion times better.

Once upon a time there were a dozen fish stalls in the market, now there are three. But O'Connell's is all you need, and is supreme for a simple reason: the brothers O'Connell chase the best fish they can source all around the south coast, from port to port, in order to bring it to the market in the finest, freshest condition. They then prepare it with great skill and care: the fish is filleted here right in front of you: no dodgy frozen fish, nothing that has been sitting around for days turning to flaky inedibility. The result is, simply, the best fish you can buy. You get the very best, then, by shopping with an open mind, and by asking Pat and Paul what has just arrived in the shop, and that is what you take home for supper. Unmissable, a part of the fabric of the city that no food lover can live without.
(Tel: (021) 427 6380)

FOOD TO EAT IN, OR TO GO:

• **The Farmgate Café – Kay Harte's lovely café, arranged upstairs on a verandah with lovely views over the market, is a don't-miss-it destination for sweet, simple and consoling cooking, excellent baking and great coffee. The foods of the market are cooked here each day, so it's as pivotal a part of the market as any of the stalls.**

• **Toby Simmonds, of The Real Olive Co, has recently opened a sandwich bar opposite O'Connell's fish stall. Needless to say the sandwiches are as cool as all get out, and this is a great addition to the market.**

• **Mary Rose Daly**

studied intensively how to make a good cup of coffee before she opened Café Central, and she is another asset to the market.

• **Standing up at the counter of Iago for a magic hit of coffee or a glass of wine and six oysters from O'Connells is one of the great market treats.**

Cork – The South West

Bridget Healy, New Zealander, Proprietor Café Paradiso:

'I've been looking for decent bread since I came to Ireland, and was delighted when I found the Arbutus breads. You have to get that chewyness, that density, and the good crust, then the butter dribbles off, and you have your little dabs of vegemite. That's my breakfast. Most bread here is so dead, it has no life, but the vegemite experience with Arbutus breads is perfect'.

● **Arbutus Breads**
At the present moment, Declan Ryan's Arbutus Lodge wholemeal sourdough bread is, for us, the finest loaf of bread made in Ireland: we are addicted! The improvement in the quality of the Arbutus breads has been spectacular, their crust and crumb impeccably tasty and flavoursome, so don't miss them, for this is utterly brilliant breadmaking.
(Available from On the Pig's Back, Tel: (021) 450 1113)

● **Stephen O'Reilly**
A legendary stall, as it's the only place you will find that great, pungent, Cork speciality, drisheen. They sell drisheen, and tripe, sell them with great humour, and that's it.
(Tel: (021) 496 6397)

● **The Organic Shop**
Marc O'Mahoney and his wife run this excellent shop, where alongside excellent organic produce you will find new things such as Tipperary Organic Ice Cream. Vital for fresh fruit and vegetables and just about everything else.
Tel: (021) 427 9419)

● **The Real Olive Co**
Toby Simmonds has been one of the most dynamic and vital people in the world of specialist Irish food in the last decade. The Real Olive Co's fusillade of stalls, selling from every significant market throughout Ireland, have galvanised the market tradition and safeguarded it for us all. Everything they sell is wonderful just as wonderful as the funky, spirited team of people who man the stalls. (Tel: (021) 427 0842)

Cork city shopping

THE CORNMARKET MARKET

A variety of organic producers set up stalls in front of the Bodega on Cornmarket Street on Saturday mornings. Organic growers such as Caroline Robinson have built up a devoted following for their thunderously good produce, so you need to be here early in the morning or everything will be snapped up.

● **Cinnamon Cottage** Everyone's favourite Cork traiteur is on the edges of the city, at Rochestown. Lovely cooking, marvellous, service, a godsend for Cork's *CCtts*.
(Monastery Rd, Rochestown, Tel: (021) 489 4922)

● **Galvin's** This chain of wine shops has several branches throughout the city and has been working hard in receent years to augment and update their list. (Washington St, Tel: (021) 427 6314)

● **Maher's Coffee** Maher's is a little Cork city secret, a small shop near to the Post Office which sells some really excellent roasts. What ever you choose will be good, but do try the Italian roast; it's outstanding. (25 Oliver Plunkett St, Tel: (021) 427 0008)

B A R R Y ' S   T E A

You will find Barry's tea for sale all over Ireland, but it remains a family firm based in Cork, and it is here that the blending takes place.
And that blending, as well as extremely particular sourcing of their teas, is the secret of the success of Barry's tea, and explains why it is such a successful brand, and why groovy stores such as Zingerman's deli of Ann Arbor goes to the trouble of importing it into the States. We would nominate their Classic blend and the new Earl Grey teas as two of the great Irish drinks. The balance of both blends, the subtlety of the bergamot in the Earl Grey, leaves any other tea well behind in second place. Brilliance.

Cork – The South West

● Natural Foods

It is the speciality breads which are baked on the premises which make Natural Foods of Paul Street such a key address. Okay, so the cherry buns are the local don't-miss-'em!, but the other savoury and sweet specialities are all just as good, so don't-miss-'em! either.
(26 Paul St, Tel: (021) 427 7244)

● O'Donovan's

Gary O'Donovan's dynamic wine shop business has a small city shop on Shandon Street and satellite branches all around the city. A good range of wines is particularly strong on the New World.
(Main St, Douglas, Tel: (021) 436 3650)

● O'Flynn's Butcher's

Simon and John O'Flynn are so skilful that even their pet foods are made with meticulous and patient care. For two-legged food lovers, everything for sale in this venerable shop is good, and look out in particular for their kassler, and for very, very fine sausages and smoked bacon.
(36 Marlborough St, Tel: (021) 427 5685)

● The Quay Co-Op

Popular vegetarian café is also home to a good wholefood store which sells organic vegetables and farmhouse cheeses.
(24 Sullivan's Quay, Tel: (021) 431 7660)

CHOCOLATES

Eve's Chocolates Eve St Leger makes some of the most yumola! chocolates you will find in Ireland. Her old-fashioned sweeties, such as Corkies and her crunchy bars, are fantastic, fun sweet things, but it is the innovations Ms St Leger wheels out at festive times such as Easter and Christmas which make her work so special: just try the candied orange peel in dark chocolate or the crystallised ginger in milk chocolate; just try the chocolate lollipops with their irresistible moreishness; just present your child with an Easter egg-filled with fresh cream chocs and see them disappear for hours into some sort of chocolate bliss. Everything Eve does reveals a chocolatier with a true gift. Don't leave Cork without several bags of Eve's.
(College Commercial Park, Magazine Rd, Tel: (021) 434 7781)

A westwards **Cork journey**

⇨ **WATERFALL**

Mrs Collins Ice Cream is one of the outstanding foods of Cork, and one of the best kept secrets in the county. You won't find it much further field than Co Cork, but on no account should you miss hunting down Tom and Ann Collins' beautiful cold confections when in the south west. The trueness of flavour, the skill in the balance of the flavoured ice creams – just taste that wild berry ice cream, made with genuine wild berries – simply blows everything else away. A fantastic food.
(Castlewhite, Waterfall, Tel: (021) 434 2050)

⇨ **CARRIGALINE**

Pat and Ann O'Farrell's fine **Carrigaline Farmhouse Cheese** is a subtle, delicate semi-hard cheese made using the milk from their own herd of friesian cattle. It's a lovely sweet, fudgy cheese, and it's mildness and sheer goodness make it a favourite with children. Look out also for the varieties flavoured with garlic and herbs. You will find Carrigaline in many shops in Cork city and West Cork.
(Leat Cross, Carrigaline, Tel: (021) 437 2856)

● The Carrigaline Friday morning **Country Market** is one of the very best, and when in the area, do bring yourself down to **Joe Karwig's** superb **Wine Warehouse**, just outside the village. Mr Karwig is one of the most admired wine importers and sellers in the country, and his range is a judicious mix of excellent wines, sold with great charm and skill.
(Kilnagleary, Carrigaline, Tel: (021) 437 2864)

 Great Irish foods to find in the supermarkets:
BUNALUN CHOCOLATE RICE CAKES

Cork – The South West

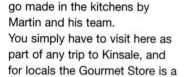

⇨ KINSALE

Donal and Laura Hayes lovely **The Quay Food Co** is a vital address in the port of Kinsale, not just for the specialist foods they sell, but also for a range of very funky sandwiches. There is always something new and enticing in here.
(Market Quay, Tel: (021) 477 4000, quayfood@hotmail.com)

● Martin Shanahan's **Kinsale Gourmet Store** is a part and parcel of his inspired Fishy Fishy Café, the busiest and best restaurant in the town. The wet fish counter here is superlative, and there are also great foods to go made in the kitchens by Martin and his team.
You simply have to visit here as part of any trip to Kinsale, and for locals the Gourmet Store is a godsend.
(Guardwell, Tel: (021) 477 4453)

⇨ KILBRITTAIN

A smart new smokehouse is the sure sign of the success of Antony Creswell's **Ummera Smoked Salmon** enterprise. But there is more than just brilliant, delicately smoky salmon to be discovered here: look out also for the utterly distinctive Ummera smoked bacon, sold in a packet with both loin and streaky rashers, the bacon is salty and irresistible.
Even the smell of it frying will have you licking your lips. And don't miss the brilliant smoked chicken – again, benchmark quality – and the fab little packs of smoked and barbecued chicken drumsticks, which are the most heavenly picnic foods. All available from the smokehouse and in shops around County Cork, and ummera.com is an well managed website with fast and efficient delivery by post. A Godsend for hard-to-choose-for relatives at Christmas.
(Inchybridge, Timoleague, Tel: (023) 46644, Fax: (023) 46419, info@ummera.com, ummera.com)

TIMOLEAGUE

Staunton's Black Pudding is one of very few Irish foods to have been awarded protected designation status.
(Spittels Cross, Timoleague, Tel: (023) 46128)

CLONAKILTY

'Clon is synonymous with a single food; Edward Twomey's legendary **Clonakilty Black Pudding**, now found in every store and supermarket in the country. Made according to the original Harrington's recipe which Mr Twomey discovered way back when, this is the pudding that made blood puddings respectable again in Ireland and raised their use to gourmet status, and you simply have to try it, and to buy it from the little butcher's shop on the main trip of the town.
(16 Pearse St, Clonakilty, Tel: (023) 33365, clonakiltyblackpudding.ie)

ROSCARBERY

Willie and Avril Allshire produce two ranges of pork products from their own coterie of pigs. There are the **Roscarbery Sausages**, utterly distinctive, unmissable. But they also sell other pork products, including fantastic bacon and sausages, under their own **Caherbeg Free Range Pork** label. These are some of the best new foods to have appeared in West Cork for manys a day. (Caherbeg, Roscarbery, Tel: (023) 48474, Fax: (023) 48966, caherbegfreerangepork.ie)

CASTLETOWNSHEND

Sally Barnes is the *agent provocateur* of Irish artisans. Everything she does, from her peerless **Woodcock Smoked Fish,** to her inspiring polemics on behalf of Irish ingredients, is of benchmark status. A Slow Food delegate, an instrumental player in the revitalisation of the markets, she is an indispensable part of the culinary and intellectual culture. (Castletownshend, Tel: (028) 36232)

Cork – The South West

⇨ SKIBBEREEN

Skibbereen is home to the inspiring **Bunalun 160** range of exclusively organic foods, and also their small and very choice shop in the town itself. Check out their site at bunalun.com, where you can shop from their sites offering essential ingredients, seasonal ingredients and gifts. The quality of these foods is superb, and consistent throughout, whether you buy Arborio or strawberry and vanilla jam. Many of the foods are also sold through supermarkets.
(Skibbereen, Tel: (028) 21356)

● Skibb is the happy home of **Field's**, which may be the best supermarket in Ireland. John Field and his team run the most brilliant store, and achieve everything to benchmark status. There is a great fish counter, a superb meat counter, every fine thing produced by West Cork artisans that you could dream of, a great range of organic foods, a good bakery, and a rather spiffing wine shop. The staff are just as devoted as the boss himself, and Field's is one of the great icon addresses. If you come to West Cork, you have to come to Field's, simple as that.
(26 Main St, Tel: (028) 21400)

● **The Saturday Morning Market** in the fair fields also brings out lots of the best local producers, including fabulous organic plants from Jean Perry's The Glebe in Baltimore (Tel: (028) 20232) plus just about all the best producers in the West.

● You will also find many good local things in **Yin Yang** in the centre of the town.
(Market St, Tel: (028) 22537)

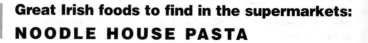

Great Irish foods to find in the supermarkets:
NOODLE HOUSE PASTA

Hudson's: What we bought

Organic carrots... home-made white crusty bread... tropical fruit flavoured fudge... Gabriel Cheese... Schull country butter... and a savoury tofu wrap to go...

● **Kalbo's** shop, on North Street, is a sister to Kalbo's Bistro across the street, and is a good source of speciality foods and, in particular, their own breads; check out the pesto bread.
(North St, Tel: (028) 21515)

● One of the vital artisan producers around Skibb' are Kevin and Rosarie O'Byrne of the **West Cork Herb Farm**. This couple have a genius for spinning out vital new foods: their green peppercorn mustard is a staple of every food lover's kitchen, but ingenious new ideas such as their cranberry and sweet cicely jelly at Christmas show a small company with endless ingenuity. Their flavoured oils and marinades and sauces can be found in all the good West Cork stores and also much further afield: just try that sage jelly: wow!
(Church Cross, Skibbereen, Tel: (028) 38428)

⇨ **BALLYDEHOB**

Gill Hudson's excellent **Hudson's Wholefood** shop at the lower end of the village is the place to visit here, not just for good foods (see below), but also to grab a bite to eat in the excellent vegetarian café adjoining the shop.
(Main St, Tel: (028) 37211)

● The most interesting local food producers are Eugene and Helena Hickey's **Skeganore Ducks**, which are very high quality indeed; you will find them for sale in shops and supermarkets such as Field's of Skibbereen, and in some local butcher's shops.
(Ballydehob, Tel: (028) 37428)

Cork – The South West

Adèle's Bakery, on the Main Street in Schull, may well be the finest small bakery in the country, and some of the breads and bakes are legendary – don't miss the lemon cake, and the white sourdough bread. Beautiful tea rooms also, and a great lunch stop.
(Main St, Tel: (028) 28459, adelesrestaurant.com)

● There is more excellent bread baked by Denis and Finola Quinlan in **The Courtyard**, one of the great icon addresses of West Cork. You will find all the local cheeses here, Gubbeen bacon, and virtually everything good that West Cork has to offer. Lovely coffee shop also, beautiful bar.
(Main St, Tel: (028) 28390)

● Don't miss Caroline Weese's shop, **Organic Oasis**, another invaluable source of good foods and wholefoods, in the centre of the village.
(Main St, Tel: (028) 28533)

● You can buy fresh fish from the stall down at the fish factory at the pier, and the choice is excellent, 'though prices are generally quite high.
(The Pier, Schull, Tel: (028) 28599)

The two outstanding Schull foods are Bill Hogan and Sean Ferry's awesome West Cork Natural cheeses and Giana and Tom and Fingal Ferguson's fabulous Gubbeen Farmhouse Products.

■ Gabriel and Desmond are unique cheeses. Extra hard, and made using only summer milk from local herds, these cheeses achieve an intensity of flavour which is simply stunning. Gabriel is the slightly sweeter, slightly milder of the two, but both are awesome.
(Schull, Tel: (028) 28593)

⇨ DURRUS

The quiet little village of Durrus is renowned throughout the cheese-loving world thanks to the benchmark raw cow's milk cheese made a couple of miles up the hill of Coomkeen, outside the village, by Jeffa Gill. For us, **Durrus Cheese** is one of the defining West Cork foods: you simply can't imagine its floral character and impressively nuanced subtleties emanating from any other part of the country. Believe it or not, but Ms Gill has been making the semi-soft, washed rind Durrus for the best part of 25 years, and her skills as a cheesemaker seem to become ever more manifest and confident with every year. Durrus is one of the towering achievements of Irish food. (Durrus, Tel: (027) 61100)

⇨ BANTRY

The **Fair Day**, an ancient market ritual held on the first Friday of each month is when you will see Bantry at its best. Lots of interesting stalls – look out for the **Crepe Stall** where Declan Ryan's superb Arbutus Lodge breads are also sold, and you can buy French preserves, locally grown veg, plus much of the West Cork producers fine foods.

▓ Gubbeen is one of the best-loved of Irish cheeses, made using the milk of the Ferguson's own renowned dairy herd. It is a washed rind cheese, with a delicate, almost-mushroomy scent and a lactic cleanness that makes it a dream date with your very best bottle of red wine.

There is also an excellent smoked cheese, smoked by son Fingal, on the farm, and young Mr Ferguson has recently turned his hand to using the smokehouse to produce the most amazing smoked bacon. In particular, look out for the maple-cured bacon. You will see Fingal with his bacon and cheeses at local markets such as the Saturday morning market in Skibbereen: don't miss this. (Gubbeen, Schull, Tel: (028) 28231)

Cork – The South West

Two Bantry Wholefood Shops

■ The produce of local growers and producers – including the rare as hen's teeth Carraig Goat's Cheese – can be found in Organico on the Glengariff Road, which is an invaluable source of good things and which also has a small bakery that produces some rather spiffing pizzas. (Glengariff Rd, Tel: (027) 51391)

■ Bantry Wholefoods is another good wholefood shop in the square that sells organic vegetables and local produce. (Main St, (027) 52611, simonorganic@hotmail.com) Look out in particular for produce from Martin and Yvonne O'Flynn, local growers and basket makers, who are also the contact for West Cork Organic growers. You can also buy the O'Flynn's produce and baskets from their farm at Maughnasilla, near Bantry, (Tel: (027) 66111)

● A few miles ouside Bantry, Manfred Wandel sells the most brilliant gardening equipment you can buy at **Fruit Hill Farm**. Everything Manfred sells combines form and function, aesthetic and practicality, and this is also where you come when you want to erect a polytunnel to grow your own food. Fantastic compost is sold, by the way, and Manfred's wife, Eddy, is also a vitally important grower, both for the local SuperValu supermarket, and for the **Bantry Country Market** on Friday mornings in the Boy's Club, her produce always meticulously grown and packaged. (Bantry, Tel: (027) 50710)

⇨ **BALLYLICKEY**

Rory Conner works out of a tiny workshop at the back of his house, beside Sea View House Hotel, and it is here that he fashions and forges the most exquisite range of hand-made knives you can buy in Ireland. Rory will make most anything to order, but do note that making the knives can require quite a lengthy period of time. (Ballylickey, Tel: (027) 50032)

The South West – Cork

● Val **Manning's Food Emporium** has long been one of the key addresses in Irish food. Mr Manning's assistance to many fledgling local cheesemakers enabled them to stay in business when their audience was smaller than it is today, and he remains the most sociable and informed of grocers and shopkeepers. The shop also has a fabulous array of wines, including many of the Wine Geese wines, those Bordeaux chateaux founded by exiled Irishmen.

Don't miss it.

(Ballylickey, Tel: (027) 50456)

⇨ **THE BEARA PENINSULA**

Don't miss the **First Thursday Market** in Castletownbere ('Castletown, to you): Real Olive Co. stall, Frank Hederman smoked foods, lots of locally grown produce and lots of craic. You can eat the local fish at Cronin's restaurant in Castletown.

● The icon food from the peninsula is, of course, the legendary **Milleens Farmhouse Cheese**, made by Veronica and Norman Steele in Eyeries. Here is a cheese as idiosyncratic and opinionated as its producers, and a ripe Milleens is one of the best advertisements for the perspicacity, individualism and sheer star quality of Irish farmhouse cheeses. Milleens precipitated the modern generation of Irish farmhousse cheesemaking, and believe us, but you will remember the first time you ever ate a piece of Milleens; we still do.

(Eyeries, Tel: (027) 74079)

Great Irish foods to find in the supermarkets: DOWNEY'S SILVERSIDE OF BEEF

The Ideal Irish Breakfast

The traditional Irish breakfast, like so many meals which have suffered the fate of becoming commonplace – even to the extent of being travestied as the "breakfast served all day" grease-fest served in so many places – has suffered because the vital importance of composing the meal with impeccable ingredients has been overlooked for many years. What you get with the traditional breakfast is, quite simply, what you put into it, so the necessity to start with the finest, freshest foods is utterly imperative. The good news is that sourcing those pivotal pork products around which the meal is composed has never been easier, for the best artisans have resurrected the skills of bacon curing and sausage making which underpin the meal. And, then, we can pick and choose the other foods we need from a rich array of sources. So, what might be a good template for making the traditional breakfast somewhat perfect. We would suggest the following as an outline:

• **A SARAH WEBB POTATO CAKE**
Crumbly potato perfection from Dublin's The Gallic Kitchen

• **MEADOWSWEET EGGS FROM TIPPERARY**
Organic standard, and available in good wholefood shops

• **DAVID BURNS PORK SAUSAGE**
The perfect plain pork sausage from Bangor's ace butchers

• **PAT O'DOHERTY'S BLACK BACON**
The Enniskillen legend, and utterly unique

• **MARC MICHEL ORGANIC TOMATOES**
Sweetness personified from County Wicklow's funky Organic Life

• **OTTO KUNZE'S FIELD MUSHROOMS**
A staple ingredient of the great teacher from Dunworley

• **BARRY'S CLASSIC BLEND TEA**
The top of the range blend from Cork's maestros
All differing suggestions welcome via e-mail: bridgestoneguides.com

Kerry knowhow

Heading to the extreme location that is County Kerry attracts singular food producers, folk who like to work at the end of western Europe. They may be at the far edge, but some are at the cutting edge.

BALLINSKELLIGS

The Skelligs Chocolate Co

There is no sweeter thing you can say, and no sweeter trip on which you can embark with your children, than to announce: 'Today, troupe, we are going to visit a chocolate factory', and to head down to beautiful Ballinskelligs to Michael and Amanda MacGabhann's Skelligs Chocolate Co.

The kids, of course, will be too excited to notice the scenery, 'though the scenery is breath-taking, and when they enter this little unprepossessing chocolate factory they will only have eyes for the tempered chocolate slooping and glooping in the vats. It's fairy tale stuff, much like the MacGhabann's own story, for they left the rigours of London to come back and work here.

In the last several years, as well as becoming media icons, they have conquered the world of chocolate, because their work is so singular, so utterly gorgeous, so blessed with an individual aesthetic. Everything is sublime.

(The Glen, Tel: (066) 947 9119 skellingchocolates.com)

 Great Irish foods to find in the supermarkets:
GUBBEEN FARMHOUSE CHEESE

Kerry – The South West

KENMARE SHOPS

■ James Mulchrone had cooked in different fine restaurants and hotels in beautiful Kenmare before he decided to concentrate on the excellent baking and day-time food which makes Jam, his funky shop on Henry Street, such a don't-miss it! destination. This place has been packed out from the day it opened, and the food shows a chef's sensibilities at work on the simplest and most vital daily ingredients. The sausage rolls are worth the trip alone, and the seed bread will bring you back time and again. Vital. (Henry Street, Kenmare, Tel: 064 41591)

■ Directly across the street, Hugo Sbeytebroot's fine The Pantry is invaluable for local organic foods and other tip-top wholefoods and speciality things. It's a charming little shop, usually decorated with a display of vegetables at the front window, packed with good things inside. (Henry Street, Tel: (064) 42233)

Cheesemaking women

CASTLEGREGORY
Dingle Peninsula Cheese
Maya Binder's fantastic cheeses have been scooping awards recently, and if you want a walk on the wild side do track down her Benoskee seaweed cheese, which is utterlyy unique. The plain Benoskee we regard as one of the brightest lights in the new generation of farmhouse cheeses, but look also for the flavoured Kilcummin. (Tel: (066) 39028 available through local markets and in Cork and Temple Bar markets)

KILLORGLIN
Killorglin Farmhouse Cheese
Wilma O'Connor's beautiful gouda-style cheeses are subtle when young, with a spiciness that increases quite dramatically as the cheese matures. One-year-old cheeses are the ones to look for, also the excellent flavoured cheeses. (Killorglin, Tel: (066) 61402)

LISTOWEL
Kerry Farmhouse Cheese
Sheila Broderick makes her hard cheeses uising the milk of the family herd, and she is the senior Kerry cheesemaker, her cheeses distinguished by a fullness of flavour and an eager texture that hides mature and satisfying tastes. (Listowel, Tel (068) 40245)

Organics

● **Billy Clifford** farms a few acres on the Cork Road on the way out of Kenmare town, and from this modest patch this modest man supplies half of Kenmare with splendid vegetables and salad leaves. It's a fantastic organisation, with the food being taken by the man himself down the hill into town each day, pristine foods in pristine condition. (Kenmare, Tel: (064) 41693)

● For more organics, contact Ian McGrigor at **Gorthbrack Organic Farm**, near Tralee, who operates a local box delivery system.
(Gourthbrack, Tel: (066) 37042)

● In Miltown, **Mary O'Riordan** organises a small organic farmers market each Saturday morning, but there are more than just local foods here, as there is also an information centre, local crafts and lots of basic animal foodstuffs and necessities. (The Natural Home Garden & Farm Centre is open Tue-Sat, Tel: (066) 976 7869)

● The best known Kerry organic pioneer is **Mary Pawle**, whose wine company only imports selected organic wines. Mary has a smashing list, always extending, always finding exciting new wines, and look out for her wines in local supermarkets and wholefood shops. Callers by appointment only.
(Gortamullen, Kenmare, Tel: (064) 41443)

CONTINENTAL SAUSAGES

A few miles out of Killarney town, off the road to Killorglin, you find the little enclave of Fossa, home to Continental Sausages. The name is rather misleading, for whilst Armin Weise does make many types of superb sausage, he also makes superb varieties of just about everthing you can name and everything you could include under the banner of charcuterie. His pates, for example, come in every style and in every grain, but are unified by superb tastes and understanding of texture. His raw meats are benchmark, and the beef olives and other preparations he prepares are stunning. At Christmas time, his mail order service is a godsend for speciality items. There is no other butcher quite like this: don't miss it!
(Fossa, Tel; (064) 33836)

Antrim knowhow

■ **HILDEN BREWING CO**
(Hilden, Lisburn
Tel: 82 884 6663)
Look out for the excellent
brews from Seamus
Scullion, the longest
established craft brewer
in Ireland, in particular
the Great Northern Porter.

■ **NORTHERN
SALMON COMPANY**
(Glenarm,
Tel: 82 884 1691)
You will find the fish of
the Northern Salmon
Company in
supermarkets throughout
the north, and although it
is a farmed fish, it is
worth exploring as the
regime under which the
fish are reared is so
meticulously thought
through and executed.

■ **WYSNER MEATS**
(18 Anne St, Ballycastle
Tel: 82 076 2372)
Wysner's is another
benchmark Northern
butcher, famous for great
sausages and for a very
distinctive black pudding.
It's a don't-miss it!
destination on any visit to
Ballycastle.

**Sausage making is raised to an art form
in Northern Ireland. Here are some great
sausage makers throughout the country.**

• **Lavistown pork sausages**
Hard to find, but worth the hunt in Kilkenny

• **David Burns of Bangor**
The perfect pork sausage

• **Owen McMahon of Belfast**
Atlantic Avenue's sausage specialist

• **Moss Brook Farm Shoppe**
Trevor's bangers are worth the trip to
Durnascallon Lane in Magherafelt

• **McCartneys of Moira**
The champion of champions

• **O'Flynns of Cork**
Sausage experimenters; try the spicy
lamb bangers

• **Micheal O'Crualaoi of Ballincollig**
We love the garlic sausages

• **Hicks of Sallynoggin**
Nine varieties, all superb

• **Superquinn**
Many Dubliners favourite banger

• **Roscarbery Recipes of West Cork**
The bangers are beautifully made by Avril
Allshire

• **O'Kane's of Claudy**
Legendary 'Derry butchers

• **Rudds of Offaly**
The pepper sausages are ace

• **Thomas Halloran of Kilmacthomas**
A classic peppery pork sausage

Belfast food routes

⇨ **LISBURN ROAD**

● Smart bourgeois Belfast is, unsurprisingly, home to the choicest shops. **Cargoes** is the benchmark deli here, and Mary Maw and Rhada Patterson do everything with an artistry and a deep understanding that makes all the foods they source and cook a true joy. Don't miss their cookery evenings, which are a real treat. This isn't just cookery: this is culture.
(613 Lisburn Rd, Belfast, BT9, Tel: 9066 5451)

● Simon Dougan's **Yellow Door Deli** has added a vital new spark to the road, and it's a model traiteur, packed with good things, another don't-miss-it! address for the best food you can buy.
(Lisburn Rd, Tel: 9038 1961)

● We seem to have been writing about Willie Browns **Arcadia Deli, June's Cake Shop, Mulholland's** fruit and veg shop and **Coffey's Butchers**, that little quartet of quality food purveyors at the top of the Lisburn Road, for ever and a day. They are still there, still as consistent as ever, still as enjoyable to visit and shop, still making people happy, and long may they continue to do so.
(Arcadia, Tel: 9066 6779, June's, Tel: 9066 8886; Mulholland's, Tel: 9038 1920; Coffey's, Tel: 9066 6292)

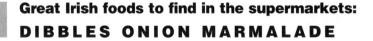

Great Irish foods to find in the supermarkets:
DIBBLES ONION MARMALADE

Northern Ireland – Belfast

Asia Supermarket **what we bought**

- **Shao Xing Hua Tiao Chiew**
- **Takara Mirin**
- **Mitsukan**
- **Cá Sac Nuoc Mam Thuong Hang Thom ngon Dac Biet**
- **Sawa Notsuru**
- **Fung Chun Vinaigre Noir**
- **Kinjirushi Brand Wasabi**

⇨ ORMEAU ROAD

● **The Asia Supermarket** is the best Asian shop in Ireland, bar none. Whatever you need, whatever you crave, whatever that recipe by Ken Hom or Yan-Kit So demands: it's all here, sold in just the right bustling, busy, noisy, cavernous ambience that you want.
Brilliant. And, shopping done, a trip across the street to the **Forever Chinese Shop** for a little authentic dim sum, and that is you all fixed up and ready to get the wok smoking.
An unmissable address.
(189 Ormeau Rd, Tel: 9032 6396)

● Just a little further up the road and across the bridge, Olivier Mandroualt's terrific **Olive Tree Company** is the place to get all your Mediterranean needs:

whatever that Paula Wolfert recipe demands, no matter how arcane or rare, it is all here, again sold by delightful staff in just the right sort of bohemian ambience.
Unmissable.
(353 Ormeau Road, Tel: 9064 8898
olivier@olivetreeco.fsnet.co.uk)

⇨ ANTRIM ROAD

Owen McMahon
McMahon's is a great address for rare meats, but as with so many other butchers, simple things such as their superlative sausages should not be missed.
(93-5 Atlantic Avenue,
Tel: 9074 3525)

Market!

The St George's Market on Saturday mornings is where you have to be – come on, who needs to lie in bed anyhow – enjoying the mighty craic generated by these brilliant food producers who have energised the market.

We Bought from:

● MR FISH
A twisting lobster from **Alan Coffey** of Portavogie

● MR JUICE
Apple and raspberry fruit sensation from Ken Redmond of **Barnhill Apple Juice**

● MR HAT
Bramley apple cake and herbs from **Glen McLoughlin**

● MR ORGANIC
Amazing carrots, radishes and greens from **Culdrum Organic Farm**

● MR JAVA
500g of toasty java from the Man in the Van

● MS CHEESE
A hexagon of cheddar 'rom the **Causeway Cheese Company**

● MR OSTRICH
Fine lean ostrich meat from **Woodlands Ostrich Farm** (to be stir-fried with sweet peppers)

● MS VENISON
Brilliant venison pies from Jilly Acheson of **Moyallon Foods**, and a pack of wild boar to go

● MR OLIVE
A bottle of syrupy olive oil from Olivier of the **Olive Tree Co**

● MRS BOILIE
A jar or two of Cavan's sensational **Boilie** soft goat's cheese

● MR WAFFLE
three hot American waffles for the children, please

● MS WILD HOT
chargrilled sausage with Boilie cheese, rocket and salsa verde from Caroline at the **Wild Hot Sausage Stop**

● MS STREPTOCARPUS
some pretty primroses from **Fiona Cunningham**

● MR & MRS BACON
blissful bacon and bangers from Trevor and Irene of **Moss-Brook Shoppe.**

Northern Ireland – Belfast

⇨ CENTRE CITY

● For speciality foods in the centre city, then **Feasts** on the Dublin Road is the address: a very discriminating eye and implicit culinary judgement from Craig Nash make this a pivotal address for food lovers.
(39 Dublin Rd, Belfast BT2 7HD, Tel: 9033 2787, feasts.co.uk)

● For bread, then Gillian Hayes' **Roscoff Bakery and Café** is the place; the standard of breads they bake remains inspiringly high, the foods they serve in the café are as savvy and smart as ever, and here is an institution that never rests on its laurels.
(Fountain St, Tel: 9031 5090)

● Just around the corner from the Roscoff Café, **Sawers** is an ever-reliable source not merely of fresh fish, but also of good vegetables and speciality meat products such as Moyallon Foods; a delightful place.
(Fountain Centre, Belfast BT1, Tel: 903 22021)

● For many, the key fish shop is **Walter Ewing's** shop, just at the bottom of the Shankill Road: great for wet fish of all varieties, but don't overlook their fine smoked salmon, which is very expertly smoked and really rather good.
(124 Shankill Rd, Belfast BT13, Tel: 9038 1120)

Best selling sandwiches from Roscoff Café & Bakery:

■ **CAJUN CHICKEN**
Cajun spiced chicken, mixed lettuce, on a ciabatta roll.

■ **PLOUGHMANS**
Home-made wheaten bread, filled with home-made chutney, and Irish cheddar cheese.

■ **FILLED FOCACCIA**
Focaccia bread filled with mozzarella, grilled peppers, pesto.

■ **BRIE BAGUETTE**
Baguette filled with French Brie, with home-made cranberry and onion jam.

■ **SALMON SANDWICH**
Fresh salmon, rocket and mayo, on sun-dried tomato bread.

■ **TORTILLA WRAP**
Tortilla wrapped around lamb sausage, humous and grilled peppers.

The Armagh couple

Thank heavens for Jilly Acheson and Simon Dougan, for between them this couple have dynamised the culinary reputation of Armagh, and brought it to the cutting edge of contemporary food culture for both specialist raw ingredients and fine cooked foods.

● Ms Acheson has done this with her fantastic **Moyallon Foods**, a company which specialises in the production of meat from rare breeds. Over the last decade, their products have just gotten better and better: amazing venison, both wild and farmed; great wild boar from their own troupe; wonderful matured beef; truly scrummy dry-cured bacon from their own pork. These are benchmark foods, which respect animal and environmental welfare to produce the most profoundly excellent eating. You can buy direct from the farm shop at their premises, also at the St George's Market, and from O'Toole's and Morton's in Dublin.
(The Farm, Crowhill Road, Craigavon, Tel: 3834 9100
moyallonfoods.com)

● Ms Acheson's partner, Simon Dougan, continues to power the smashing **Yellow Door Deli**, in Portadown, and has recently opened a second branch on the Lisburn Road in Belfast. This is an archetype delicatessen: great foods sourced and cooked with care to be taken away, excellent comestibles for the larder and freezer, and a great catering service. You will also find them at the St George's Market on Saturday morning: don't miss the venison pies. Be smart, and let them do it for you; they do it better than you can.
(6 Bridge St, Portadown, Tel: 383 53 528)

Down Ulster way

BANBRIDGE

● The two key destinations in the town with the curious Main Street are Jim Quail's benchmark Deli and Butcher's shop, **Quails,** an essential source of wonderful foods and great local meats.
(13-15 Newry St, Tel: 4066 2604)

● A little further down the street, the **Windsor Home Bakery** has lots and lots of those lovely squishy breads and cakes which locals, and visitors, love.
(36-38 Newry St, Tel: 4062 3666)

BANGOR

● **David Burns** George and Brian Burns now mastermind the late David Burns indispensible shop, home to what may be the utterly perfect pork sausage. Everything they sell is good, and for Christmas their bronze turkeys are worth ordering – as they have to be – from November.
(112 Abbey St, Bangor, Tel: 9127 0073)

HOLYWOOD

● **Camphill Organics** Sadly the bakery in this visionary organic shop is no longer functioning, but it remains a great source for John McCormick's singular, definitive organic vegetables, as well as for various wholefood specialities, including great home-made humous.
(Shore Rd, Holywood, Tel: 9042 3203)

KILKEEL

● **Whitewater Brewing Co** Producers of a hard-to-find real ale.
(40 Tullyframe Rd, Kilkeel, Tel: 4176 9449)

MOIRA

● **McCartneys** George McCartney's butcher's shop in the centre of pretty Moira is not merely the definitive butcher's shop, but one of the definitive shops. Everything they

source and prepare is of benchmark status, and, as sausage-makers their more than thirty varieties of banger are quite simply astonishingly good. Don't Miss! varieties include chilli beef, gluten free (for those who need it), pork and leek, pork and banana.
(56-68 Main St, Moira, BT67

OLQ, Fax: 9261 1422, Fax: 9261 3533, mccartneysofmoira.co.uk)

NEWCASTLE
● Sea Salt Delicatessen
Carolie Fitzpatrick's popular deli has good food to take away as well as to eat on the premises.
(Central Promenade, Newcastle, Tel: 4372 5027)

ELITE GUILD OF BUTCHERS

Northern Ireland has the finest butchers and the best butcher's shops you can find. Here are the elite of the elite:

• **A Flanagan & Son**
1 Scotch St Armagh, Tel: 3752 2805

• **T Knox & Sons**
388 West St, Portadown
Tel: 3835 3713

• **Mr Eatwells** 16 Campsie Rd
Omagh, Tel: 8224 1104

• **The Quality Food Shop**
7 Ballyclare Rd, Glengormley
Tel: 9083 2507

• **David Burns Butchers**
112 Abbey St, Bangor
Tel: 9127 0073

• **Norman Hunter & Son**
53-55 Main St, Limavady
Tel: 7776 2665

• **McCartney's of Moira**
56-58 Main St, Moira, Tel: 9261 1422

• **Owen McMahon**
3 Atlantic Ave, Belfast
Tel: 9074 3535

• **J E Toms & Sons**
46 The Promenade, Portstewart
Tel: 7083 2869

• **John R Dowey & Son**
20 High St, Lurgan, Tel: 3832 2547

• **E R Jenkins Butchers**
41 Main St, Ballyclare, Tel: 9334 1822

• **McKees Butchers**
26 & 78 Main St, Maghera
Tel: 7964 2559

• **O'Kane Meats**
69 Main St, Claudy, Tel: 7133 8944

• **Turley's**
57 St Patrick's Avenue, Downpatrick
Tel: 4461 5333

Fermanagh the cure

O'Doherty's Butcher's shop has been trading in Enniskillen for more than forty years. Whilst they have always been respected for excellent Angus beef, fantastic burgers, and as sellers of venison and game, and whilst their sausages have followed the standard course of winning numerous awards which the butchers in the North seem to manage so effortlessly, it has been Pat O'Doherty's recent quest to create the style of bacon which was normal when the shop first opened that has attracted the plaudits of food lovers.

O'Doherty's dry-cured black bacon, made using a secret recipe which sets it apart from their normal dry-cured bacon, is a masterly food, with superb texture and flavour, and with none of that ghastly scum which extrudes from conventional bacon and which means it is, in effect, boiling in injected water rather than frying. Best of all, you can buy it as fat, medium or lean (we'll have the fat, please: fat for flavour as they say in the trade). And don't worry if Enniskillen is a long way to go: they will send it by mail wherever you are. "Famous For Burgers" it says on the front of the shop. They will have to make the base of the front wall a bit bigger and write "Famous For Bacon And Burgers" now.

(O'Doherty's Butchers, Belmont Street, Enniskillen,
Tel: (048) 66 322 152, blackbacon.com)

Foods Ireland should be producing:

Air dried Ham... Artisan Cider... Farmhouse Cheese in Northern Ireland... Crab Apple Verjuice... Heritage Variety Tomatoes... Bottled Raw Milk... Cider Vinegar... Mutton... Waxy Potatoes... Air Dried Beef... Sea Vegetable Products... Pré Salé Lamb... Brawn... True Country Butter... Boxty... Irish Salami... Franchised Farmhouse Cheeses... Heritage Variety Apples... Cured Ham... Mature Co-op Cheddars... Apple Brandy... White wine...

Derry the inside track

Food lovers make their way to the little **Moss Brooke Farm Shoppe** at Trevor and Irene Barclay's farm at Durnascallon Lane, **Magherafelt**, to get some of the very best bangers and bacon you can buy in Ireland. Like many other farmers who produce pork, the Barclays were almost squeezed out of business by collapsing prices, so they have turned to selling direct to food lovers, via local markets, the St George's Market in Belfast, and via the shop. It's a logical step and a successful one, and don't miss these exceptional foods.
(6 Durnascallon Lane, Magherafelt, Tel: 7963 3454)

● And in **Magherafelt** do yourself a favour and head straight for Robert Ditty's exceptional **Ditty's Bakery** on Rainey Street. Some of the things Mr Ditty bakes are pure benchmark, none more so than his amazing oatcakes,

which are vital – indispensable – with any cheeseboard: these are superb. But care and tradition shine through everything here, which makes both this shop and their branch in Castledawson don't-miss-'em! stops.
(33 Rainey Street,
Tel: 7963 3944;
Castledawson, Tel: 07946 8243
dittybky@aol.com)

● In **Claudy**, on the Main Street, **O'Kane's Butchers** is home to two of the most talented butchers in Ireland. Brothers Michael and Kieran O'Kane are thrilled by the challenge faced by the modern butcher, and they pursue their vocation with passion.
Their meats are exceptional, but it is the cooked foods you will find here, in particular, which are superlative: no other butcher makes a pie as good as these guys, so put Claudy on your vital food routes.
(69 Main St, Claudy,
Tel: 7133 8944
mail@okanemeats.com)

Wine lovers

Northern Ireland is also home to the most dynamic wine merchants in Ireland, merchants with superb wine lists and services.

• **James Nicholson** and his team, of Crossgar, have won the award of regional wine merchant in the International Wine Challenge so often that you might reckon they would relax and take it easy. Not a bit of it: Jim and his team criss-cross the globe ceaselessly for fantastic new discoveries, and find them with a regularity which borders on the unbelievable: every time a newsletter comes through the door or is sent via their benchmark web site, there are brilliant new bottles.

The shop is also a most gorgeous wine emporium: step in here and say goodbye to self-control! A wine shop and a wine merchant who quite simply improve the quality of your life.

(Killyleagh St, Crossgar, Co Down, Tel: 4483 0091, jnwine.com)

• **Compendium** wine merchants is another spiffing shop on Alanbrooke Road (which is extremely difficult to find in BT6, so call for directions). Neil Groom takes care of front-of-house, and the list and service are both super, with high standards simply taken as the norm. We're still intrigued by the CD Compendium

sent out when they first opened, a quartet of tunes accompanying images of denim, boules, sex and rugby. Lateral thinking is clearly the order of the day in Compendium, or maybe they came up with the idea at the bottom of a bottle of Barefoot Pinot Noir?

(Tel: 9079 1197
www.compendiumwines.com)

• In Belfast, the McAlindon family's **Direct Wine Shipments** wears its years lightly and seems as youthful a business as ever, always extending its range with new discoveries (South Africa most recently), whilst remaining very strong indeed in the regions of Spain (a particular passion) and Italy.

(Corporation Square, Belfast, Tel: 9050 8000)

• The newest kid on the block for wine lovers to take note of is **R&R Wines**, run by Robert Neill. Mr Neill and his team are Australian specialists, and whilst this is a young company, there is passion for the vine aplenty here, so expect to hear a lot more about R&R in the future.

(Ell's Fine Wines, Dobbin Road, Portadown
Tel: 3833 2306 Fax: 3833 6326)

Second generation

The 2nd Generation Artisans: Bred in the Bone Hell, why should it just be in business that family dynasties are created. Ireland's artisans have begun to put their sons and daughters to good and profitable use in recent years, so here are some of the young blades looking to expand Mum and Dad's empire.

FINGAL FERGUSON
@ Gubbeen Farmhouse Cheese

● Fingal Ferguson has taken over the smoking of the sublime Gubbeen cheese, and extended his profound skills with Pinney-style smoking to make brilliant smoked bacon. Don't miss the maple cure!

DICK WILLEMS
@ Coolea farmhouse Cheese

● Young Dick Willems now makes the most profoundly sweet, buttery, the-aftertaste-just-goes-on-forever! Coolea cheese, up near Ballingeary in North West Cork.

PAT & CATHERINE MAHER
@ Cooleeney Camembert

● Pat Maher takes care of marketing Cooleeney and Dunbarra cheeses, whilst sister Catherine has become the principal cheesemaker on the Maher family farm in Tipperary.

ED HICK @ Hick's Butchers

● Everyone knows that Ed Hick, of Sallynoggin, is the finest pork butcher in Ireland, fewer folk know that Ed's dad, Jack, started the business many years ago. Other great butchering dynasties include:

Second Generation Artisans

BRIAN & GEORGE BURNS
@ David Burns Butchers of Bangor

● Son Brian and cousin George run the same meticulous show as the late, great George.

JUDITH McCARTNEY
@ George McCartney Butchers

● In Moira, a younger generation of McCartneys has already begun to add to the raft of trophies won by George McCartney over the years. Daughter Judith is actually the 6th generation of McCartneys to run this astonishing shop.

JOSHUA, LOTTIE, JACK & JIM
@ Skelligs Chocolate

● Alright, so Joshua, 11; Lottie, 7; Jack, 5 and Jim, 2 MacGhabhann are still in the junior set, but just wait for these guys. They already help out with painting the fabulous boxes which grace the wonderful Skelligs chocolates, and despite his tender years, it is Joshua who already has charge of the children's page on their website – www.skelligschocolates.com.

BILL DWAN
@ Dwan's Brewhouse

● Bill Dwan is one of that exciting band of micro-brewers who are shaking up Irish brewing, with his funky bar and brewery, Dwan's Brewhouse, in Thurles, Co Tipperary. But Mr Dwan has the advantage of continuing and developing the business of a family with several lifetimes spent in the drinks industry.

NEIL GARVEY
@ Biddy Early Brewery

● Another second generation brewer is Neil Garvey, of

Second Generation Artisans

the Biddy Early Brewery in Inagh, County Clare, who now brews the brews in this characterful brewpub.

ANDREW RUDD
@ Rudd's Bacon

● Andrew Rudd has taken over from mum Prue and dad David in masterminding County Offaly's superb pork producers, now operating from a state-of-the-art production factory.

JASMINE HYDE
@ Ballymaloe Relish

● Jasmine Hyde shows the same sort of brilliant judgement in the making of her Ballymaloe relishes as mum Myrtle Allen has always shown in running Ballymaloe House in East Cork. Just check out that jalapeno relish!

TONY BARRY
@ Barry's Tea

● Son Tony has the helm of Cork's benchmark tea blenders; don't miss their Earl Grey tea, which shows every other bergamot-scented brew a clean pair of heels.

THE NINE CLEARY BROTHERS
@ Glenisk dairy

● The Cleary brothers have transformed the old Tullamore Dairy run by their dad into one of the country's most exciting organic operations. Don't miss the organic rhubarb yogurt.

index

The Bridgestone 100 Best Series

• THE BRIDGESTONE
100 BEST PLACES TO STAY IN IRELAND 2002

This is the most authoritative and up-to-the-minute guide to Ireland's finest hotels, country houses and bed and breakfasts.

'No-one who drives in Ireland, north or south, should travel without a copy in the glove box of their car.'

THE SUNDAY BUSINESS POST

• THE BRIDGESTONE
100 BEST RESTAURANTS IN IRELAND 2002

The Bridgestone 100 Best Restaurants in Ireland 2002 guides you to the most creative and cutting-edge restaurants throughout the country.

'When you read and use the guides, it is impossible not to be deeply impressed and to ask yourself whether, these days, Ireland might indeed have one of the finest food cultures in Europe.'

THE GUARDIAN

• HOW TO RUN A RESTAURANT

In this provocative book, John McKenna offers a radical analysis of how restaurants operate, and why some restaurants succeed where others fail.
Examining the business from the position of a customer and a critic, McKenna analyses the factors which contribute to success, and explores the decisions which have to be understood by anyone who is either already running a restaurant or considering opening a new restaurant.
Practitioners and students will find the book an exhilarating intellectual exploration of one of the most mercurial and fascinating industries and entertainments in the world.

'The McKennas are the most powerful food writing team in the country. They are exciting and talented critics.'
THE SUNDAY BUSINESS POST

The Companion to this guide is...

The Bridgestone food lover's guides to Ireland:

The Traveller's Guide

● The Bridgestone Food Lover's Guides to Ireland – The Traveller's Guide tells you succinctly, wittily and accurately who are the best cooks and innkeepers, and where they run the best places to eat and stay throughout Ireland. Everyone wants to be on the inside track, and to have the vital local information: here it is.

● The Traveller's Guide is for the resident who wants to know the best places to eat in their town, city or county. It is for the traveller who wants reliable and accurate information about the places they visit right throughout Ireland. It is for the tourist who wants to discover the magic of Ireland's food and hospitality cultures.

● With humour and insight, The Traveller's Guide describes the very best that Ireland has to offer, from grand city restaurants to remote places on islands off the coast of Ireland, from boutique hotels to cosy B&B's, fromsimple breakfast stops to cutting-edge cooking.

● The Traveller's Guide simply tells you who and what is the best. It is not a factotum of Ireland's tourism industry, which feels obliged to list each and every place to eat and stay. Instead, it is a highly critical, highly selective guide, which unveils to the traveller the very best that Ireland has to offer.

● And in discovering the very best that Ireland has to offer, you will discover one of the most exciting, inspiring food cultures in the world.

'For the last eleven years they have specialised in directing visitors away from the clover-leaf edition of Ireland and toward the modern country inhabited by the Irish themselves. And, in producing these guides, this ebullient couple show real hospitality in inviting visitors in Ireland to join in the chase.' **THE LOS ANGELES TIMES**

Up-to-the-minute news
and any relevant changes
in the Bridgestone Guides
can be found by visiting...

bridgestoneguides.com

VISIT...

bridgestoneguides.com

and sign up to Megabytes, the free
newsletter of the Bridgestone Guides.

FEATURES INCLUDE

- **Up-to-date information about the world of Irish food**

- **Regular campaigns to protect our food culture**

- **Monthly recipes**

- **A look at menus from both Ireland and abroad**

- **Features and recipes by some of Ireland's leading chefs**

- **Readers' letters**

- **Competitions with great foodie prizes**

- **A free noticeboard for the trade, buying and selling anything from a front-of-house to a side of organic pork!**

PLUS

- **The Megabytes Club!**

- **Special Offers!**

- **Irish food and wine ordered directly through the web.**